The
Hexagon

Robert Kelly

BLACK
WIDOW
PRESS

Boston, MA

The

Hexagon

Robert Kelly

Joseph S. Phillips and Susan J. Wood, Ph.D., Publishers
www.blackwidowpress.com

Cover photo credit: Charlotte Mandell

Design & production: Kerrie Kemperman

ISBN-13: 978-0-9971725-1-5

Printed in the United States
10 9 8 7 6 5 4 3 2 1

α

RAZO

Hexagon: a six-sided plane figure.

But we are children, so we've got to get our hands on mathematics, touch the numbers. I crumple those six sides together, pull them into dimensional space, and find a cube in my hands. Six sides plus five fingers make a cube.

Something like that.

Something about sixes. The mystery of six. Mystery of sex. Sixtus in Latin, the sixth of something. Sexus, sex. What is the link, the beehive of connections from which we grow. Pentadactylism is general in the animal kingdom, Olson reminds. But there is a six here somewhere in us. Six is Sex, the thing that makes one two, and makes two one. *Druk* in Tibetan means six, but also means dragon. Shall we guess at the dragon? And that sound in Russian means friend. How close a friend. Close as the sides of a Platonic solid, the Cube? Hex in Greek means six, but in German witch, and in English the spell she casts.

The Hexagon is a poem made up of six-sided stanzas. These stanzas are meant to borrow some of the properties of a cube, each face of which is invisible to all the others—at least the outer sides are. But who can know what goes on inside the cube, and what the inner faces might look like, or what they might behold? Each line need not look backward, or gesture forward.

Each side of the hexagon (= face of the cube = line of poem) must be in some sense complete unto itself. It can't even *be* a part (as of a cube) unless it is a whole, intact unto itself. Thus, each line must be complete—the author is aware of some of the ways in which a given line can be complete:

1. It can make a statement. The statement could sketch a narration, or express an idea, and thus impersonate an ethical or spiritual proposition.
2. It can offer materials for thought—images in disjunction out of which the glad mind of the reader gets stuff to work with or play with. Matter.
3. It can propagate and abort syntactic sequences, hurry to a meaningful gap.
4. It can offer an image to haunt the mind for a while as the reader reads on—thus managing to temper time.
5. It can start a story rolling. Because a solid beginning can rule a myriad of possible continuations, the vaunted completeness of the line will then take place or entrain in a time perpendicular to the poem.
6. It can be taken as a command which the reader will properly resist, and perhaps find the struggle illuminating. A hope.

The frequent aborted syntagmas and giddy discontinuities are perhaps influenced by the powerful scission in Lacanian analysis — the sudden cutting off of the session that throws onto the patient the whole brunt of making sense of what has been said, what is even in the unfinished act of being said. All to make sure the complete line is not finished.

A certain number of three- and four-voiced fugues occur within the stanzas, occasionally identified, more frequently not.

In Kabbalah, five is Gevurah: severity and Mars and war, while six is Tiphareth: splendor of sunlight, empathy, alchemy and peace. It is the author's aspiration that hexagon will dream an antidote to pentagon.

— *RK*, September 2013

1.
What kind of animal has me in its mind.
Who is that in my mouth.
Make the sound of someone speaking.
I love you so much I share I.
The catch of the glee assorts the owl's hour.
Spring always needs to talk about wings.

2.
Be kind to too the things outside.
Tie shoelaces to the trees.
Down in the cellar the black light goes on.
Infamy of riding coats our poor fox deceas'd.
Children dawdle to school grownups drive by them fast.
Things you notice how the keyboard cheats.

3.
Shadow of the bowing arm stains shirtfront.
Is there a nearby animal to speak.
Varicose profits in a downturn hum.
I star my cable box delete to who.
This is of course how it yearns to speak.
Come back loving or come back all.

4.
Use me every day or silent night.
Red string caught in bush doth bird delight.
Do the colors change from year to year.
Does red always mean what I said.
He drives in blue a paper cup to church.
May Day the green is almost donned.

5.

Marxism a primitive form of global capitalism.
The proletarians won but the proletariat is very small.
The masses now gainfully unemployed.
Tax cap veto laws are the rosary beads of the rich.
Politics is the opiate of the intellectuals.
I wanted this to be just for you and me but.

6.

The almost of ever is for you too.
Rebound pedestrian from the sunside of the meat.
Light is the purest aggression.
Trees teach us to wear clothes.
The crystal structure of sugar's unfathomable cube.
Substance is pure mystery aren't we.

7.

Water comes dripping out of a book.
You're not rich because you have money you have money
                                        because you're rich.
Suppose we keep pace with every season.
We Tuesday gulp our oatmeal porridge quick.
Of course this is an island.
You can't go the distance without getting wet.

8.
Everything means something else as well.
That is the problem with water and oceans more so.
Sunday jogs but bless relaxes.
Care for I share don't mean me.
Look at the cost of that old car.
Moneychangers in the temple stubble on my jowl.

9.
The sloping of the maid.
I'm tired of religion it has to lie down.
Frictionless intercourse the maiden's smile.
Not Caravaggio but mother naked anyhow.
Thus I refute approximate shadows.
Without knowing what the word means.

10.
Scum the light leaves behind.
Three women in black dresses pull people's legs open.
Mean mind me she all is mind.
Taking a risk all this is about.
Sit on the sink and hear the mirror.
All the famous women of the safe search off.

11.
Suddenly the sun at midnight.
It is well to live past your witching hour
The book opens to an unfamiliar alphabet.
From the open book strong light falls out.
Light has a tendency to come down from.
We have a tendency to be some kind of ladder.

12.
A good grump from Mon morn.
Cherokee as me is hardly anybody.
Nip nose of fave niece.
When in doubt abbreviate.
Cherry pie ripens in a novel's stained leaf.
Bric-a-brac at Saltonstall's buy boutique.

13.
Goshen ponies wonder where they're headed.
In tall rows of wheat men hunt for chaff.
Grass over head top the sunlight whiffles.
We need someone to whistle the wind up.
Feebly remember Shostakovich on 50th Street.
Children in these days sang in the road.

14.
Which was the other way when it began.
Always the alternatives contrails diffuse.
Bad child ignoring mother's piña colada drinks milk.
But which future is the one we have.
There is a line that leads there crisp cotton of its flag.
Blood comes here to be cleaned.

15.
Immortal ones can understand the gap.
Given an operation using land and air brutality he.
A kind of infestation like a clock.
Sometimes the warmth Avestan scriptures argue.
High pitched laughter as a sea bird knew it.
Take a deep breath before your profile shows.

16.
Come up here pretend to be a lap on a listener.
I used to read the papers in my sleep.
The fish of miracles swim upstream in the dark.
When we remember animals our souls are comforted.
Church suppers for the unruly poor.
I flee the mother of my current infatuation hide.

17.
This is certainly the same as where I come.
The bottom of a barrel stained with olive brine.
Luwian alphabets strung across the Bosporus.
Ishmael was black I tell you Ishmael is black.
Aeneas and his Trojans became Etruscans not Romans.
The Romans came later and killed them most.

18.
You learn to read by thinking against the words.
Think against whatever they tell you school.
Utterances of gnomes who live beneath the grind.
One thing after another light through a billion windows the
                                                    same light.
Hear the yearning spoken in the shadows corner of the room.
A shadow knows everything of form and music a shadow is
                                                    the same as time.

19.
God is the mirror of our best intentions.
More live compassion towards all beings.
All living things all entities ever thought.
The closer we come to the brightness in the mirror.
Such things we dream and wake to scribble down.
Try to catch the shadow of the Speaking Angel.

20.
Furies are as hard to catch as angels.
Sinuous a-slither in black around us in us.
Called The Kindly Ones because they live in us.
They're named Compassion Kindness Wisdom.
They rebuke us when we fail to out the best in us.
When we fail by failing to acknowledge failure.

21.
And rain comes from the sun.
The king of a thing stands up.
No government confesses it does wrong.
Maintaining the lie is the machine that wrecks it.
Think of half-penitent Oedipus uncitied.
Think of what it means to lose the people's will.

22.
What can I know about these moral things.
Always wanting onward no more sprocket holes.
Stay away until another say.
Change a blue habit into mindful plum.
Organ voluntary fills our empty stories.
Lissome listeners float *a capella*.

23.
Hear for once with your own ears.
For a child everything is miraculous in us.
Expectant stillness in soft air.
Two birds my tinnitus.
Storm soon under noon.
It breathes out from this very rib.

24.
Bones of Samothrace in three jars.
One jar for each god the house is full.
Everyone's a skeleton inside that's why.
One-finger exercises beat the broken drum.
Sailorman reef your distances.
The horizon is no nearer ever.

25.
Was I sculpture or was I another thing.
The silk rose in Lucite water aids eternity.
Everything sounds a little like something else.
And that was a rose too.
Loving a person's name but not the person.
Endstopped allegro over the frontier.

26.
Always someone waiting.
Why is *waiting* first think morning thinks.
So many days breed one desire danger.
Until they only need to use their thumbs.
Idle on the lap remote control warm knees.
Syzygy and wake the woman let her go.

27.
Any act at all compromises power.
Me was the hairdresser skeptic as before.
Once men wore leather soles in this broad town.
Now we use their skins to patch the sky.
Past centuries leave healing dust behind.
Cocktail of cremains liquefy newed muse.

28.
Swallow the evidence of Bayreuth and Berlioz.
Catullus's bones resemble scented talcum.
Grind and reuse to rouse the unemployed.
Skydiver Biber violin astringent tea.
The long quiet opiate of work begins.
What is the be in before and behind.

29.
To have an idea hard work for the hand.
Things work as hard as they have to.
Bring peace at last to the calendar.
No need for time the princess sleeps alone.
That halo round her head is human hair.
Adobe mansions ideas are more like rain.

30.
These are patterns in the dust love decides.
Lute night in northern cities an accident in doubt.
Because you said it she reforests her belief.
By dulling their ears drink makes people listen.
Through the words and in the trees if ever.
There was going to be gone and only he to go it.

31.

Neglect the obvious for once it's sticky from your love.
Interfolded fingers press the thumbs together up.
Do the dead know when their names are spoken.
Do the living know when a friend's thought thinks them.
Are there enemies at all or just more animals.
Wild turkey down this little hill steps mumbling.

32.

Can you say one thing only and still go on.
If this were a question you'd have to be an answer.
I believe in what men feel when they say that word.
The awe of other and the mirror bright.
Lie in the sand and make long demands.
Seafowl are glad to message thee.

33.

Does not know where last year's go.
Deer meant any beast one time ago.
An animal is pure demand.
Welfare is wild fire.
Skimmer top and idle August seldoms.
Yearned and yearned but never learned.

34.

I was the spindle of a clock a face forgot.
You were my Palestine a stone house.
Measure by fervor the faith of the subject.
Dire is a beast in thicket or wild swan.
All overheard by night a little left.
Cry to the night and morning answered.

35.
I spell my way a different time.
Her viola climbs the tenor stave.
A sound *seeks* music *flees*.
Everything has much to say but less so we.
Her face was wearing mountains on May Eve.
There was a worn spot where the skin showed through.

36.
One claimed to know the body from the shape of nose.
Every logical proposition is a Mohawk war canoe.
When you're in the forest you're too close to argue.
Come back to Monday to be born afresh.
When you're crying you sound just like a New Yorker.
Only the sun is sitting on that bench.

37.
So many things to you.
Exasperate the obvious one more time.
Things often break when they do.
It's not fire comes out of the sun pure information is.
Museums close on Mondays do they fear the moon.
What is itself the explanation.

38.
Seek the hare but hide the hound.
A witch lives in your shoe.
Mother green and father blue let little little world be read.
There is an animal inside I think.
This *ba* bird takes the soul away.
The soul I speak's the soul the *ba* bird takes.

39.
Each thing is itself and something else.
Salt and pepper snow on gravel.
Customs fetched back from the Indies.
No time for clocks in this puce cheek.
Spank naughty mothers who won't leave child alone.
They claim that bats are living in my joists.

40.
Soft elbows are too long asleep.
Write or play the piano nothing else he said.
Organ grinder lease your monkey to the wind.
Let me tell you weather's no free lunch.
We pay for every pleasure and even more for pain.
Soulish people say whatever comes into their heads.

41.
The girl who reads the meter trains the light.
We are trapped in the evidence of thwarted felonies.
At least let me hold your scarf while you shiver.
A sneeze is a confession of complicity with the outside world.
Note down her offenses in a little book.
After a while the book becomes your heart.

42.
Any book at all how long you wear it.
This is true if even that is also.
Fewer jays less aggress but hawk or two.
I have to keep explaining my job is.
Bees explained Trojans supplanted by Etruscans.
Nobody knows how to read a poem anymore.

43.
Now I don't have to think I have to be.
There are workmen in the clouds suppose.
Too little traction to be legible.
Arrogant interludes of making sense.
Easy meaning like easy virtue.
A bird could do it if a bird could fly.

44.
Remember that far ahead.
Now the rhythm is all in thinking nothing heard.
The deaf snake does not fear the music.
Songbite a bitter prophecy a tune to come.
Now I leave you joyous in the present land.
She hides in my vocabulary.

45.
The size of being kind is being kin.
The other side of this only place again.
To be born is where the rest is when.
Forgive me narrative's a broken egg.
I called for music and geology appeared.
There is no logic like the Swiss frontier.

46.
Follow the hero's tracks in the no.
Somewhere has been here before.
Someone has drunk strange water and said grace.
It was empty till you came.
Closets full of nothing but remembering.
I was empty till you came.

47.
Restoring each of us to our begin.
Again the traffic's quiet bay at always evening.
Weather inside the clam shell what shall this flower.
Entropy means loss of heat my word cools down.
How to open things came all our meat.
Children remember former lives by touching things.

48.
Things My grace and goodness shew She cried.
Because a mercy means us and no mildly.
The boat cracked and the fish came out.
Origin of animal life on earth to make a mineral speak.
Sleek limbs then the concert of them when I think.
Neurons kneel down at Isis her name.

49.
To be born by water or a bay is to be held.
Meek habit of all days before.
Now inspan the bigamous steeds of the Apeiron.
Climb the harvest and let it chariot.
Weigh far more than we suppose the animal.
The part I love is always waiting.

50.
Always saying thank you never sure to whom.
You I know but is the you I think the you you know.
It doesn't matter much of stone to utter thanks is all.
Rilke says our only job is praise itself is chemistry.
Stuff the rough cloth into the copper athanor.
Things love being suddenly together.

51.
Silence language so that it can speak.
We cut the levee to let the meaning blur.
Will is the opposite of paying attention.
Listen to the color red and ask no questions.
It tells you everything if you listen.
This whole animal is called permission.

52.
Listening affirms no matter who speaks.
Clouds are the loudest part of what we art.
Trees full-fledged early May when will you fly away.
Walk on the steel grill over quiet hell.
A doorway says it all the whole house just listens.
In my confusion I know the clouds know something.

53.
You're never alone when you have a sky.
Numbers began one day when men were too tired to think.
There must be more to me than this.
One extended oneself and so two was four.
Too tired to think men could only count.
Logic like self-abuse satisfies and nobody gets hurt.

54.

The great thing about language comes so many ways.
Blue pole barns under obsequious cumulus.
Charles Sheeler went to heaven heaven is not far.
A house is the strangest work of humankind.
All at once the numbers were all gone I had to count
                                            something else.
Bees tuned the girl's piano the window glass was on fire.

Cold that music was and dead men hummed it.
All consonants no vowels the language of the dead.

55.

Why make things bigger aren't even small.
So little of the eye sees what is blue.
Narrative repels desire narrative is anxiety.
Learn what you can't ladies not what is told.
How good the telling to the teller how old the told.
Don't hear me darling just listen to me.

56.

Now I am ready to begin he thinks to see a tree.
How can we repay the old poets Kalidasa Sophocles.
It is measure keeps us moving.
Over the hill is Italy and they say springtime.
Over the hill is a rock with no meaning.
Birds at the feeder know all I mean.

57.
Grateful inadequacies that keep us sane.
A line is long enough to reach silence that's all.
Birds in the soffit region nesting nesting.
Inner word compels us to compel.
That all is silence is.
Speak like a spinnaker wise from afterthought.

58.
What is moral got there from the ground.
I knew the ones that loved or other flame.
Who cares what I think some what I say.
The middle of something is always again.
Cut your finger wonder how anyone can kill.
Terror needs no logic gives no milk.

59.
Don't know whether I'm alive or dead.
Went through the white mouth gate and fell.
Tile is baked but why always cold on my skin.
Every picture is a doorway to come through.
Everyone you meet is a door to open and go in.
The tree inside hangs heavy ripe with fruit.

60.
Green rooves decisive evidence.
Talmud falls open here Tractate Levanah.
When the moon fell down on the town's green rooves.
Dogs worried the bodies of dead soldiers still do.
The Church built churches still avail stones teach quiet.
In those halls you hear your not-self think.

61.
Overactive pituitary induces trances.
This particular trance is called the way we live now.
Enzymes take care of things by themselves.
Men build bridges over rivers the king's deer swim.
I don't know much about living but this is now.
Physiology is the thief of time.

62.
His lovers missed all the small disorders.
Something crackling in the canteen a cliff falls.
A plover dabbles wingtip in wet sand.
Lead me away from my nighttime.
Into music's atrium where rain is meant to fall.
Orchestral density my heart on fire.

63.
Not any name suits animals they need new metal.
A cup of maybe with a slice of hope.
The phone rings in the Vietnam War I answer.
We are far from what we need is seed.
There is no earth left the sky won out.
The world is a mineral with windows in it.

64.
Things add up to lily mornings then.
From lilac blooms an earwig fell on my hair.
This sunset hour to privilege prone.
Again the light and again the light and again.
Call for harpy comfort and skin comes too.
Aligned with the obvious so no one wakes.

65.

Yellow buses drive them to the obvious.
Count the noons and multiply by minnows.
Hurry the river the stars are impatient.
Pedagogical value of silence absence night.
We need to be meadow before we wake up.
Blue glass mother-of-pearl an ocean.

66.

Don't think it let it lip it leave.
The sound of a thing is closer than the thing.
Exhausted soldiers in flooded barracks.
Elements in disarray thanks to human passions.
They think through us pestilence tornado.
Wanted to hear but the light was off.

67.

Your eyes staring at me from the heartwood.
They listen best who leave before the end.
Carry the unfinished with you your life completes.
Bridges go nowhere that is their secret.
You can't cross what's gone Styx all round us.
In a Slavic wheatfield someone's standing.

68.

Now the news hath filled the belly with the wet wind.
Leaves of sunlight represent the trees.
Help me with the names of things again.
See through the earth and beg the ones beneath.
This all is true and tree and wonderbeast again.
Because I was new I got things right at last.

69.

Marks in clay remember bleeding men.
We mean less when we weep hard heart.
Bird in the roof strange zoos colonize humans.
Castaway a century ago still in damp clothes.
Bide a beach a beam swivels and falls floats.
Ragged but regular a regiment of knives.

70.

For lore lingers long as bodies feel.
Tree craft and low arriving drink from your hat.
Once in the street they never come back.
Nowhere further in the world than here.
Mow the lawn the lawn mows back.
A tree's a machine for standing there our teacher.

71.

Aberration I want to bring perverse to you.
Hermetic backsides of the Marais.
Put me to sleep so I can tell.
In trance my advocate in dance your magistrate.
Listen to me try to meddle my footsteps with.
Mourning dove! low murmur voice of grass.

72.

Barely coherent who at the most of times.
Cogent phylacteries damp upon your breast.
Peacock my way through your syntax solo.
Old rock related to a troll by marriage.
Around the night cape with bell and chimera.
Be thee for me and I by replication thine.

73.
Lamb on the table turns wise eyes within.
The tree inside keeps talking me.
Ancient raga of martyrs' reliquary brass.
Touched each other's in the library.
I am the book you always never meant to read.
The gleaming aster foretells the end of time.

74.
Sound of a kickstand supporting someone's wheels.
Orchid from Peru she brought me in the dark.
Outside the Blue Mosque thunder's after us.
Evening insects unfurled interview your state of mind.
Policy comes after cathedrals men forget women never do.
I know everything as long as I don't think.

75.
The back door to come in remember-music.
Hymen was the littlest god ruled all the rest.
Where the crow walks the rain must remember.
Isolate in underwear when the daylight failed.
Verbs don't tell to whom or why but you.
Academics gaitered in long-march polity.

76.
A star in heaven crosses someone out.
Light itself is hyper-focused silence.
If we were really silent we could see everything.
Robust chanticleer impersonates encyclopedias.
Speak soft to baffle dormice on the roof.
In thatch to catch all wit to weave.

77.
Well the wit be on us now.
Scary blue beginnings poets blather of.
Blerwm blerwm on their lips-harp.
Some strum some keyboard folderol.
All that is child's play and outworn.
I would be further from myself.

78.
In bed with color I need your art to carnate in.
Another body for this beast this ghost of mind.
Every prayer portends an explanation.
Listen soft and let me let me the old man cries.
For he is living in this forest still.
Kind to children but his mind on else.

79.
Give art your all and art gives all you need.
Lap is such a magic kind of politics.
And there things be enough to tell thee.
Climb my tree if you dare espouser.
A line from hither meets a silver gap to yon.
Every question is an accusation.

80.
Every question is a naked man.
I thought I heard speaking but it was shadow.
A question is always an aggression.
In this country midnight learned to talk.
What can you do with what comes to mind.
Or swallow the bitter juice of silence.

81.
But why is someone sleeping in your hair?
Now be lilac where everything is the time is cool.
Fools think spring is some kind of an answer.
Catching line drives in the outfield fast asleep.
Pitch darts by instinct in a darkened room.
All done with burdens with a belch of ease.

82.
There is a better word for any given thing you see.
Shape it in your hands until it is like your remember.
Terrible moment when I smell me in the dark.
Because it is fright really as old Melville said.
Ishmael was a colored man Ishmael was black.
Only on board a danger are all men brothers.

83.
Our sea is blind and stretches out cold hands.
Some white thing makes captives of us all.
Feeble colonists on bank-owned fever coasts.
I love it when you watch the men at work.
A harpooner must be my kind of man.
Suppositious caravans bemused by sand.

84.
I will find thee bedded in the rock my dove my inscription.
Reading you I learn who in fact I am.
Don't start talking when the words come close.
Where shall I tell thee where the body does.
In grain of wood to read all history.
Stalks of chard and mustard vegetable bones.

85.
Imagine these lines inscribed in stone.
Pinky syenite of Egypt word after word.
The sun is the moon's mind-night fantasy.
The sky is our skull turned inside out.
History skulls in green cenotes limestone pool.
A city is a dividing who can drink it pure again.

86.
Find the secret point where the open starts.
Public space begins inside any word.
Windows look out on a broken street where does the heart
                                                        begin.
I wish we were finished so I could begin.
They rhyme with their shoulders they dream with their knees.
Glassware nested in raffia crated from else a war ago.

87.
I dream the blue house who am I.
Love is micromanaged or love's lie.
The car starts the bird stays song is like that.
The story never begins two maidens play on metal harps.
 I saw the face of the volcano roaring stone talk.
Try to understand the meaning of the turquoise rosary.

88.
Can't be closer than to come.
Irrawaddy spillway wets a gory dagger.
Bring war home with you till we say no.
Eden reopens when no one kills.
What an easy way to win a whole new world.
Angry brother fingers unclench his rock c'est tout.

89.
Mixed signals lose battles clash of register banners trail in mud.
A woman's voice among the tenors climbs their staff.
Call it opera because it works down deep inside the ears forgot.
Merciless listener reads abandoned reference books.
In heraldry three wolf heads cut off and one nude corpse.
Ads show us all the crimes we did and fled and lingered in.

90.
Thetis smiling out of her wet clothes.
Grasp northern gods by knobs of both their knees.
Every god is from the arctic every god needs sun.
The sun was my sister and I had no mother.
We come out of each other street by street.
The further away you are the deeper inside you.

91.
Always new-ward axiom seek tell me.
Swan-ward yelping comfort the desolate hotel.
Chanting the Heart of Wisdom Sutra over and over.
The cloud disperses its molecules persist.
We breathe the mist of foreign prayers alien poetries.
Batter my heart open old oaken deity.

92.
Drag the line draw old Jerusalem.
Where a sparrow is bigger than a hand.
Fly me to the other side of your eyes.
Not to be seen but leaves by wind away.
Not just it but everything is moving.
Wood lets you talk about her all day long.

93.
I mean your matter who is shaped of light.
I have erased my longings in order to belong.
I have caught a hawk and flown a tiger free.
I have had intercourse with equinox and who was I.
I have eaten fruit from an agony tree.
I have someone else's blood flowing in my veins.

94.
Then the summer stopped and the poor sky broke.
Credited everything heard caution metallic sodium.
Who scared the dusty dog who built the chair.
They wound a human chain around the destined town.
He spoke that very day the No One of the north.
Green my counsel and a postcard from your mom.

95.
Hospital for the healthy this old world is.
Rank on rank the redcoats came out of the mist.
We talk about color but it is not the color.
It is not color that works on us but the beings who ride
                                        on color.
Color is *vahana* the steed that Being rides to reach us.
Who are they who do who are the riders of the blue.

96.
Where was the looking when I was.
The hen pheasant crossed the road before the road was.
I followed her into the yearning a body is always.
I will have my way with time I thought I owned her.
But there was flying to be done an altitude of clothes.
White white like the bosom of a waterfowl.

97.
Beyond comparisons a need for sleep the pillow damp.
Damaged citizens relent against their systems of belief.
Trust one if that blame nobody at all all molecules deceive.
Changefulness in waiting in the chambered heart variety
                                        is silver.
Packed like words together in a meaningless remark.
Betray yourself with passing woodlands you are no king of.

98.

Perilous describing the roots of mankind fathomless.
Where do you get off when I came in on random avenue.
We are made to stand on corners and not be sure.
What was who thinking when I woke or what.
Geese come down and walk the cornfield clean.
Reflect your self until enlightenment.

99.

Or could was have been a pirate queen abaft of longing.
Was was a lingerer a glance over whose bare shoulder.
There is no was or some sort of library locked in the sea.
Falling from the mouth a cataract of sense my Egypt lost
                                                    as well.
Troubadour manners a sack full of white-throated sparrows
                                                    loud.
All things to do mean done all done things lost in never.

100.

There are places where we sleep and come again.
High up La Chaux among six-horned goats One Taste.
Cumin is culture this is remembrance this is umbrella in soft
                                                    rain.
Standing in an empty field filing his nails an emperor after all.
Come back from Gaul your caverns full of mute excitement
                                                    stored.
Don't you even know you are the earth you walk upon.

101.
Don't you even know outside is inside and a dream.
What does your hand remember of all you touched.
Too many lights can't a man die in peace goodbye little name.
We come down from heaven to occupy hollow spaces in your
vocabulary.
All you need is break the rhythm let the light sound in.
Summit of thingliness his heart in flames displayed.

102.
There are beasts but what does it mean to be blood.
Study beech trees to learn what wood actually wants.
This man can't tell a woman from a tree.
Everything in the world turns into one of them.
By Cavaillon bronze age bones exposed in mud bank.
A broken skull what does time want of me what does time
want.

103.
We walked down to see the ancient bones.
Lifted her into the wind she never came home.
Crackwitted servitors of a dead idea.
With dry fingers it crumbled the Renaissance.
Half a lot is more than smoke or is it fog.
Fledglings falter down the sky inside.

104.
Where everything matters is the rule of three.
Photographers clustered ready by the opening door.
You found me in your peace and offered fish.
Simultaneous Samothrace hooded brother overnight a god.
On the day Knife something drips from the branches.
Poetry is the portfolio of the very poor.

105.
Carry these with you to the unpromised land you make.
This loves you because this is truly this.
How can I make up for all she's lost because of me.
Love made me and the hours began then and the horses.
Hide emeralds in grass where do rubies hide.
People in that country will say anything.

106.
Tense in neck and shoulder this is writing.
Writing is scraping body tensed into gouged matter.
Purple heather writing is matter.
The state is a kind of ink that blurs and blots.
When do we begin the puberty of our race.
No one was listening so it sang again.

107.
Porphyry slab inscribed with illegible.
Could I be the first eyes that saw this stone.
I wanted to be there before myself.
See what the world is like without me.
Ethics of desire let the other go.
But another one was waiting after all.

108.
Other other be my pal now nobody smokes anymore.
Spoke into the volcano vanished in a fume of word.
Breakfast broke lunch lurched dinner didn't.
I come from the tar pits to call you home.
Bones in ancient gravy birds in ancient sky.
Horror follows clefts desire led the way.

109.
But what do they like the ones who make the trees.
Meat from no lamb wood from no tree Atlantis rises.
The world ends every day that's the miracle the proof.
Is it evil to love the lips more than what they say.
Art is what does nothing but makes them think.
Art is what makes them think.

110.
Riding the sunshine rain.
A beam of light leads you through the woods.
These are variations on the simplest things.
Coptic letters midrash on never-written scripture.
Speak like you mean it like a dog barks.
Maybe you even know what you mean.

111.
On a fairy island like this a willow's tree believe.
Who is I to be telling whom what or ever.
Break the habit of light the lamp burn air.
Nothing diminishes a man more than himself.
When you have finished it all listen to the light.
You're what I've been trying to tell you.

112.

Kiss it to be new again a buccaneer.
Licked the bowsprit of time succumbed submerged.
Under the keel of earth a millimeter silence flows.
Ritual sunlight touch the wheat narrative begins.
Bang the door softly the bears sleep their only honey.
Touch your wrist and tell my time.

113.

When the sun's not shining there is no color red.
O I am tired and new and need not much to say.
But I was a salmon then a badger and dead besides.
Now the definition of human body still waits its cup.
A woman asleep beside a sleeping lion and no moon.
The stone lion finally spoke a Russian song came out.

114.

These are the bees that toil inside everyone.
The rose gives honey to the bees the chatter of thought.
Fill your street with my shadows let them overlap.
Angels with leaky watering cans drift down the wind.
Wallow in virtue like a full-page ad.
Unclean vowels breathed in the god house o woe.

115.

Churches deep comfort frog-green altar cloth.
The hum of light baffled by sainted glass.
Absorbency needed too much rolls off the mind.
Cloudable mercy on the schoolhouse roof alight.
No more school now it's just learning all the time.
Inside the healing walls no sound but you.

116.
To have come so far not sure of having left.
The phone rings in every cloud
We are gored by ancient astronomy the sky.
The edge of things is best since closest to between.
Leap into neighbor sky hope the bees are home
Each point of light a synapse in our guess.

117.
I am an empty room what is your name.
A myth that flowers tell: light grows from shadow.
Any deep woods tests your grasp of grammar.
She buried a book in the ground so it grew inside her.
If even one word slips all the bridges fall.
She crouched and wrote her finger name in mud.

118.
In this room we keep cloud in this a peculiar sound.
Housekeeping is hardest for the head.
The hero's habit is to cleave the hardest word.
The bridge goes nowhere but a harp in air.
Pyrenees roadblock briefcase full of loss.
Forgive the mile no man can go.

119.
And if I were finished with my work what then.
Would shaman reclaim her tundra and the wolf.
Some things suicide themselves when we neglect.
I raise my voice to the Lord of Hosts there is no just war.
Stop killing is all we have to do there is no just war.
Start with not killing humans for any reason no just war.

120.

Bees desert the hive when time is wrong.
When the world ends it starts right up again.
Never doubt your prophets just doubt what they say.
Prophets serve the truth by telling lies.
The universe ends a million times a day.
Things break when we stop loving them.

121.

I speak nonsense because good sense kills.
Anxious to be bees he split himself in sixes.
To find the woman in the sun the burning amber.
All the world is different kinds of sugar.
Crystals analyze the history of things.
Travel the axis of the invisible to the real.

122.

We can take any name we please but will it listen.
Loins of Egyptian goddesses conceived geometry.
Men grow old by owning things.
We betray childhood by having children we become the enemy.
Too many pictures to be safe on your mattress.
Stare right through the color and see her face.

123.

There were a dozen Eves who made a million Adams.
The secret name of God is you.
A sinner with no sins a temple with no priest.
But what if it's the letter that gives life.
What if we are alone on this curious ship.
God is a pirate who interrupts our dreamy cruise.

124.

Gnomes gather shadows faeries restore it's raining.
It's not rain on your skin it's a blue jay crying.
Disturb the obvious and pay the price.
Theology without belief I preach the god of praxis.
Know god by being god as you know love by loving.
At the end of belief you can almost see the real.

125.

What shall I do with your breath I breathed in.
There is a temple where such gods are served.
Breath rearranges words so bodies can hear.
My lungs wash your breath it leaves a residue like pearl.
The roots of words lie deeper than feelings.
The word came before the thing it names.

126.

From our first words the air was born.
Vowel song to voyage truth among the living.
Open your mouth when you come to a door.
All a house knows how to do is listen.
Sometimes an empty room begins to speak.
Knothole in clear pine shows the other side of time.

127.

So many genders so many doors.
You live a lifetime before you know which is which.
Life is a confusion with soft green leaves.
I am a man but not the kind you mean.
A horse be hobbled by his rider's hope.
Bathe me clean again with your only breath.

128.

Irises behind my house the color of them in sunlight.
That is the whole epic one line says the whole war.
To notice what we see to speak our only liberty.
Mystical chatter of angry squirrels up the trees alas.
I used to believe in nature too but then.
Let God believe in me he cried and someone meant it.

129.

When in doubt water the flowers.
Phlox dutchman's breeches spiræa drizzle.
Air is a week of its own turning but to whom.
Who does this turning every ask an aggression.
Breathe for me little valley every leaf a breather.
Body listens but spirit nills there is no bridge.

130.

There is the Spain in you the bridge is broken.
When you sit on the lap of the wind what does it whisper.
Poetry exists because death does it is the only answer to.
There is a fireplace in heaven no one by it but the cat.
O what a beast it is that sleeps so many lives.
Wake the door to wake the street the street runs away.

131.

Not sure how far away is far from I am.
Name you after from the star-rose when you cried.
Measure is everything but it measures nothing.
Wilderness of thinking along a dry river bed.
Immortality a glint of blue the night sky a gleam.
In our language we call this you.

132.
The gleam in the shrine room led me in.
Night after night same light on different me.
Hide my laziness in non-stop labor.
Hide my silence in so many words.
There used to be a rooster crowed next door.
Time is kinder than neighbors kinder than sunshine.

133.
Fierce mystic text each line a testament.
Of those who go down into the subways do all come out.
Every cave beneath the earth is the same Lascaux.
To go below the ground restores human to system default.
The information flows past any possible point.
She talked six hours in the chestnut tree.

134.
Take me home with you to California the way the sun does.
Something like asking for help something like dream.
Strange green animals that live on light.
The number seventeen makes people dream it worries me.
As if everything were alive one immense subjunctive.
Raise your glass if you remember your first word.

135.
One day we'll sex with angels and a new race come.
Whatever you're reading now is a list of past lives.
An uphill treatise in a thousand books beginning here.
A purchased paperthin pilgrimage air of Ladakh.
Textbook of arcane geometry the nine-sided feminine.
You are a harp strung in an open doorway body sing.

136.
Nude door harping on heath giggle of herring gull.
Chant the sound of coaxing angels who are they.
Humans ontological chauvinists think they alone have minds.
A jackal does hard work he thinks his pleasure.
Wet silvery streets of Atlantis soft with traffic.
They are coming to invest us are in my mind right now.

137.
If you get really good at it you'd better stop.
Arrowhead finial on Gothic choir stall.
Facility is the enemy of craft.
Each wife had seven sinners in her hell.
Part two blades of grass and there's the gate.
Not so many stories but more of them than us.

138.
Green serene of morning just before the sun heals.
How to be done with things and wear a cotton rag.
How to go to church and not be there.
How to lift a woman's arm across the room.
How to leave folk snug in their own wills.
How to ask for what you need beneath the want.

139.
The old woman scolded I wrote from desire not from need.
Nothing has no color and that's my problem.
In a world where nothing can be repaired.
Brain always waiting on the corner for the mind.
If I told you the truth would I listen.
Enough to think the names of colors and quietly weep.

140.

You see where this is going the man in a tree.
The years are wrong from starting over and over.
The tree is permanent and the man may be a woman.
Feather jabbed in the sun an eagle's almost bodiless scream.
All loudness and no volume an idea out of the new.
We wait on the jetty for a crime that never comes.

141.

The mind coming now and never left home.
Four quarters to the heart but one for you.
The Blood doth teach us Numbers and the Air to breathe
Augment interact environment fondle irises.
I wanted the way you walked down the street.
Ten thousand voices make single thunder listen.

142.

My scepter has tarnished and my pavement cracked.
Remind me what good story is but isn't ours.
We are the unnecessary animals of earth becomers.
Through our eyes you lose sight of what is there.
The room's swept clean behind my back.
Houseboat on the Herrengracht and a smashed guitar.

143.

Show all the acts with line drawings no color and no shade.
By line alone to sue intricatest narratives aloft.
Any line leads eventually to silence that's what beauty means.
A wife a minute all along the way and then.
Affect into autumn sky fades the cloud letter A.
Then the silence listens to you and you are.

144.
Right hand rests natural in left hand it makes a lap.
You are in her hands of the mother.
Watch what she shows you eat what she gives you.
Cloth feels like nothing it's not on her skin.
She lives on the other side of nature but so do you.
Nature is her shadow and yours too.

145.
Green chair on green lawn and no one there.
The human voice is an afterglow.
Resilience means expect no help.
Thinking would work if there were anything to think.
Un mot et tout est perdu means poetry.
It is rare to hear a house outshout the words.

146.
The sun winks at me my head confesses.
So many saints on earth none left for heaven.
How dare you speak that yellow way.
If I don't help you I'm fooling me.
Anyone dervish thickens the air itself.
Asclepius his grove a mere woods heals.

147.
Throw a word out in the world what happens.
Whittled wood Oregon porch Sunday.
What did you see up the skirts of the sky.
The traffic comes down from sunlight.
The truth you tell is the truth of bone.
I looked into her body and saw another country.

148.
Only with reverence to speak geography.
A landscape copied in us saw her proper dreamlands.
Springs and her groves and rock the sea not far.
I am a bride when I get lost in you maybe oriole.
Sing in the shy woods so a lady'd ask me.
Tell what love is and why it hurts so hard.

149.
Wine on the stoop and a mad priest raining.
Swear oaths instead of axioms to shame the archons.
Enraged he clawed the sympathy right out of the music.
Naughty children speculate a dirty mirror.
Splats of gyzm on the locker room floor.
Love is not that or not just that or not that yet.

150.
Blackbird goldfinch purple finch this is the key.
Ancient equation we have to solve every day.
Silk rose and two real roses this is the secret
A child drawing lines in wet sand is the secret too.
There is only one everything and everything knows it.
Listen to them getting the lake under the launch.

151.
A lambscape and hide in the thicket gold gleams far.
Sun caught in branches do dare to set it free.
Let things go and follow till they peter out.
You'll see the children nailing shadows to the ground.
Who are the old men who stand around the pump.
Now you're at the hipbone of the story the horse neighs.

152.
Strange tall steeple on Hudson uphill house.
The sky cries out at such poignarding grace.
Here you see with closed eyes your heart's desire.
Screw the bulb in backwards give the dark a chance.
When you stare at the sky something opens.
It shows you something you have never seen.

153.
Stranger to this planet unknown weights and measures.
We move things by thinking red hospital on skyline.
The heft of things I'll never know it all feels wrong.
Feels wrong to carry the body's meant for something else.
Something else muscle something else pleasure tears and milk.
In a land without effort the mind at peace.

154.
Don't write it down yet ink will drown the poor thing.
Let it gasp in the mindshine an hour to grow strong.
Chipmunk leads us to the middle of the maze.
Two rosa rugosa right here but where is the sea.
Cavorting with miracles the world forgets to end.
Believe what's in your mouths and he's already come.

155.

Resident inquisitor this leaf looks at me.
I love the way wood gets wet for you.
A hummingbird for all I know.
It has to say everything or nothing at all.
This need I mean the profligate hours.
So long it takes to say so little one whole life.

156.

I am not who you were the first of time.
Angel of over plead her garments on farewell.
Learn Latin again or Jove weather licks you.
This dragon never sleeps no priest can dwale him.
To have lived before and after a person's whole life and still
                                                              be me.
Extension ladder clanks closed bring down the noon.

157.

Workmen clamor at reluctant toil Chinese.
The truck backs out the bird goes by.
Sit quietly with things and they will tell.
A moon of sixes for a child to come.
Real kisses not finicky frenchy bisous.
The great mystery lost inside our clothes.

158.

Now's the time to look at everything.
Smooth galloping calendar white horses past.
Leave your shadow in the turf and come away.
Some body inside everybody's middle-aged.
Spell it out like a Christian don't make us guess.
Amber lamps do honor to bared flesh.

159.

Don't move anything see it just where it already is.
Radical economists trip over clover fall.
I lived round the corner from they danced in the street.
Because he had come again who never left us.
Dancing seemed the deepest kind of prayer.
Endurance means turn hard somewhere be like stone.

160.

Running so far and not brass a circle of gold.
I was a horseman in the winter raid she summoned.
How can a child know the size of what to do.
Opera is the parody of alchemy that gets it right.
It changes you wordless in the behearing.
Not the story but the strain of voice in effortless.

161.
Every grown-up is a villain there and no one sleeps.
To make it better only makes it worse poor Robespierre.
Gather round I'll tell you what the blackbirds told me.
There is room in heaven for the sky for humankind on earth.
Gulls on the outfield grass in Wrigley Field make matter clear.
We thought this whole thing into place now think our way out.

162.
Little more than a girl she read my cards for me the tower fell.
I read her palm and named the children she would have.
There is no bitterness like being right.
I pray for the mercy of blundering drowsy dawn's geometry.
Tall linden left with few leaves to count the days I say.
We tried to make music while the master slept a different key.

163.
Three roses now one woodchuck eating torma.
I must be getting better the music stopped.
All I ever mean is listening out loud.
No more tragedy trim your fingernails.
When people are ready to answer the sun.
How far does light dare carry us after all.

164.
A twitch in the fingers spells a different word.
Code switching natural we live on earth a while.
Elsewhere once and then again real home.
Something seems right here something strange.
The human face is a Potemkin village.
Nothing there but nothing here.

165.
I want it to be better but it's me.
Tile table beside her empty chair is Samarqand.
Look for the dreamer lopsided flower.
Momentum of attention weigh the meats the measures.
Webs of response bear me down she strikes within.
Emerge in intellect what slept in will.

166.
Nothing See should be the targe.
The trammels of misfortunes cloak the grace.
Amazed by intellect he falters in love's couch.
Embattled periwigs excruciate the law.
Are we all like that a game with no wings.
Near to the lastness an ear decides.

167.
The little bugs that manufacture summers.
A tenderness try not to kill abase the will abase.
From A to Z Antarctic emptiness.
This book was never written this word was never said.
Negative spectrum with rose in the middle.
I saw the green end of the universe it sang with me.

168.
The drill bit sings into the willing steel.
Grind far dear friend you bird in the far.
A litmus lady mine Air turns blue.
Scupper drenchy ankles of the silent king endure.
Waiting is like wading but the wet is dry.
Far fling like a game without a pilot lost in reeds.

169.
Sly questioner a vast forgetting slops my thought.
Tillage and the rights of swine hock and lavender.
Documents annexed to Roman road blue clay for dinner and
                                                    a fish.
Real estate is worry the rest just keeps the rain off.
Without some game to play we could not lose.
You owe a lot to the law for such comely sin.

170.
Never far from Provence his eagle slept on lofty currents.
Best adamantine vantage to spy the needling elvers.
Life inserts itself in every cranny that's all it ever means.
Probate of a cousin's will a wealth unknown divide us
                                                    strangers.
People alas belong to the other side of need.
Money in the bank the church on fire.

171.

Obsession sucking milkweed maid asleep in sunporch touch.
Could any linger after so long skin on skin as if.
Somehow was supposed to be wet and went away.
Could it have been the lake dream swim with foxes.
We grow up through unawareness thick around us.
Where did the angel go is the empty question.

172.

Cast about for an alternative method of prolonging life.
I found my pet white rat under a lamp on 23rd Street.
Why did you leave me here so many years ago.
By now I have had a thousand generations of descendants.
I'm still waiting for you to come back for me.
Any beast you borrow is a Bible for your life.

173.

Things stay with you when you pick them up.
There is no tragedy like connection things never let you go.
Open the gates of the human heart.
See the strange brass idols on service there.
Hear the organ try to sing a single human word.
Why is every word some other.

174.

Always a day late and the eights lopsided eternities
Morgan slept below her spinnaker barely a name.
Who came caught who fled desired.
There are moments and there are movies.
Look away from the image and see.
See in your lap your purse is bleeding.

175.
They bore him comatose their drowsy schooner west.
He will wake up with love in another image.
So busy in blond sunshine the much-talking street.
Look on them as kittens playing in the sun.
Everyone tries to make a private dream world public.
This vain attempt is culture economics *Homo ludens*.

176.
From far enough away I look like a nice person.
The worst fate is to be trapped in your image.
The monk in his summerhouse tries to climb out of himself.
Crime is marriage a prophet dancing on a burning hill.
My father's nickname for me was Rasputin.
Locked beneath the ice I saw eyes open floating north.

177.
Lion light of angry springtime.
Write every day and you'll write for eternity.
Born before Hollywood and fed on clams.
Judgment is itself the basic crime.
There is no such thing as law only paying attention.
The untranslatable freedom of maybe.

178.
O liberal death who unlocks so many personhoods.
Bring close to the fire to see far away to understand.
Skandhas indifferent there is nothing there to lose.
Locked in the physical by a taste for skin.
Forgiving wall being close to wall being smooth.
If it were only it and I were I again.

179.
Someday I'll learn what the truth is about.
Fix facts in amber set ideas deep in leaden cloaks.
Trapped in image trapped in clothing trapped in skin.
Came close to where we were supposed to begin.
Breeze makes everything bearable first evidence for God.
We ran out of barbarians and had to become them.

180.
No actors in no play no stage just justice naked.
Appearance in a sky that seemed to speak.
Believe don't belong hold troth not trust.
It took so long for you to get to know me I was gone.
Broken stadia bones of a giant howling sea wind.
Everything in either Talmud is right here.

181.
Unbuilding the wall is a glad too time.
Molecules unsinewed from their too-fabricked ranks.
And nothing stands and nothing falls the breath is all.
Prise ivy from old wood the light shows through.
Yellow fever days mortared bricks with wet sand human hair.
You live as long as you keep unpiecing the wall.

182.
Three strokes of unmemory the hand is glad.
Nothing to open a door to nothing to keep out.
Memories are sheer fantasies resemblances impostors.
I thought about hypotenuse and the hidden earth.
This must be done soon mother is it not.
No answer worth such a noble question.

183.

Cost of cars my caravan of salt.

How many moons crowd one small sky.

Hawks harry beasts too comfortable on earth.

No cries in the cathedral kneel to sleep the sleep called prayer.

Hearken to lust arouse a sudden opera storm of dry moth

wings.

Beat around the window chapter of dark words.

184.

No truth in what I say the only truth is saying it.

I hear the edge of things the crumbling headland.

Don't think coherence solves the problem or desire.

How to be quiet enough to hear is enough of all.

Timing is everything and there is no time.

I learned that language yesterday but now.

185.

Lost the lucid in the scout parade.

Things come into being through mere attraction.

Flood the deserts with nutrient guesswork.

Bring the moon a little closer and fake rain.

Cherish the distances between things.

Distance is love it is the only of.

186.
Things look at us from the woods.
We are not privileged with their thinking.
Too many of us in one story love them.
How long we've wanted to tell them so.
Patch of sunlight on the lawn their valentine.
We say je t'aime with tears in our eyes.

187.
Nature we used to live in that town.
Nothing happens every island is like this.
We wave our arms to bespeak a maybe mainland.
Night fog to keep us snug inside the Ark.
The flood never ended we're waiting for the crow.
We thought it was laughter it was waves was birds.

188.
There is some music to this kind of forgetting.
Till we touch fact in each other every name rebukes.
What are we here for if not who are you.
Does any island need us.
How many of them are ready to be us.
Religions turn cruel as they grow old.

188.
After you break the glass where does the light go you let out.
Everything you see belongs to you.
This is the secret name of the ocean far away.
Roses gone this morning someone nourished.
It always wants to be somewhere someone else.
Sticky skin can we live on honey.

189.
We still need need still desire desire.
Reach out and help the getting there.
When I grow to the level of my predestined work.
Watch how close she is across the room.
Drowsy watchman on a hillside south of sheep.
Move the man and let the lady in.

190.
Her whole body speaks a language I don't know.
A red fox ran across the way home.
Every word is an anxiety disemboweled.
The boredom of secular vice.
Wait a minute all I meant was sunflower.
All I meant is what gives itself unasked.

191.
Is there life still in the old measure.
Is a month long enough to go on.
Not so many trees now the sun has taken.
That other circumstance the rabbis told the *sparkle*.
Never think it is what it looks like and you'll be safe.
Things talk to you that bale of hay's a grizzly.

192.
Have you listened once too often to the rock in your pocket.
Anything worth believing is worth talking to.
The text lies sleeping in the fountain pen surrender serenade.
The unrolled scroll is blank! I can read everything.
Scattered tesserae left when the mosaic's done.
Each one is its own color that is what matters.

193.
Colors last when the narrative is gone.
See the light that looks at me the children's book begins.
Amalgam of bees and Beethoven frantic wisdom school.
Read your Roman history for Christ's sake.
Men with weapons steal taxes from the poor nothing changes.
Something else really needs to happen here.

194.
Hold back the weather the man is rising.
He is tired of what isn't stone and doesn't sing.
Why do I always have to do all the talking.
It came with the farm a wishing well or mill.
Artesian poetry by weather suck secret water from the earth.
Windwheel manners I am kind to strangers.

195.
Where is the rage in all the little days.
Caught sleeping by the rim of the sun woke.
La Brea walked a girl from Ilion with auburn hair.
The personal is always oil essential plumeria wreathed.
Sanguine poetics of the sugar industry disarm.
Give these islands back to the sea!

196.
Measure witch cords string islands together.
As far as I can ever tell Oahu.
Lispings of prisoners in my soul vault who.
Most of it is allegory the rest just hurts.
Glasses for sale that see the about to die.
How many stones stumble a given afternoon.

197.
Princedoms of the lower air friendly neighbor us.
I came without my interpreters to rule by guess.
My own language is a friendly magistrate came by mule.
Adjectives come right out and love you from far off.
Lovelorn seneschal a man on fire why not all women mine.
Lock the chapels the sinners are coming.

198.
Can I wait for all those meek beginnings.
We who define happiness as the morning.
But the morning is your actual skin.
How can you drink Kona with so much sunlight in it.
Because the chaparral is full of bees.
The skinny new moon whispers Spanish.

199.
Having things to talk about and having things.
Wood presses leg flesh stars hurt sky.
Nothing but contact everywhere but the distances remain.
Alternatives are interferences there is only one way.
84000 directions walk the same road have I heard.
We are proud to come and come again but where are we.

200.
Leash makes lust law makes sin we know all that.
These stars are stairs but they go up and in.
Sit on the steps and feel your way down.
Basement light flickers every house Lascaux.
Those are our red hands pressed to the wall.
Ocher of the inheritors teeth of the windowsill.

201.
I live in a skyscraper no one can see.
When you're finished with me at last snow in Paris.
She slept behind the wheel but I was driving.
There are seven seas Water Air Dark Light Conscious
                                        Memory Death.
What I learned in school was to hate school.
School kept me from learning kept me from books.

202.
It took me so long to listen with respect.
How else does love linger in a silent earth.
Ask more of me and less of it there's Gan Eden.
Can I get my language back before you go.
Dismiss this I-ing personage this mummer from the
                                        Holocene.
We Irish stand on our heads to dance.

203.
Every book a new religion.
Let adequate strive to be superfluous.
Minnewaska naked cloud no rain small river.
If you can remember a single tower you'll be saved.
Intricate intercourse of tongue and object.
No one ever ever knows enough.

204.
The spear of Woden baptized in Christ's blood.
He had no lasting business with the sky he's here.
Wherever there's a lake you'll see him sometimes rise.
The pagans kept Christ alive safe with us in Avalon.
Master of the Word spoken by no one word outside time.
Secret Christ inside the Baal Shem Tov.

205.
Or anyone at all the miracle persists.
Retain the obvious it rhymes with your life.
The function of rabbits is a function of lawns.
Snow scurf in Paris I woke afraid the boat the boat.
I am he who told you he was not.
Know the best lovers study Ancient Greek.

206.
Where are you going with all this I've been and gone.
It's here now like anything else all there is.
Nothing kills a wish like getting it.
Childhood shul a sycamore tree a simple hat.
They shaved their heads to feel the sky.
Pagan people are always at home.

207.
Carloads of circumstance and one spray of lilac.
Late for the season violet in the graveyard.
What Proust knew and what he didn't.
Princess tree they say flowers before leaves.
I sit beside you lost in the wedding trope.
Over Berlin a skin of uneasy light.

208.
How many children to no school.
Hypotenuse of desire mystery origin of fugue.
Linger at the philtrum kiss the unremembered.
In wet clothes in Canaan *bosheth* is shame.
Erase the radicals and the scriptures disappear.
Caught in moral languor like a beach on fire.

209.
The senses six rehearse our tragedy all day long.
Those who worship images eat nothing but images.
Linger at nape nerve and breathe you my truest word.
What have you done to me I am alive.
Every mother is Doctor Frankenstein.
Shimmering parts of shame decode as genesis.

210.
It must be philosophy if nobody understands.
A reef a rock a riff *anguis in herba*.
Today's intellect takes the form of glare.
Flaunt them when you're young then hide the key.
If only the way of the world led to the world.
Translate your body from Ancient Greek your house.

211.
Working hard to be a man a minute.
One tree silences a whole sea.
And should was burned away by maybe.
White wood white wood be my god.
What I wanted to say in love with your material.
Filling the ocean a priest for supper.

212.

Blue novels of the Sanhedrin matter is your mother.
Keep things near the wood will love you.
Gull in cloud ram caught in thicket cherish.
We did not come into the world to be understood.
The fathermother is the first and final mystery.
They made me and I know not who they are.

213.

We stand the same sea the same shore.
You run up naked over the stones to me.
I slap you gently on the hip you pull my hair.
We are children together there is no world.
Never adults we grew in not up.
We are so close no way we can be together.

214.

Glaze of day mild spilt milk descending.
An argument of birds interrogates some seed.
Rock-handed interpreter brother strong lifts against hollow.
How do you kill an emptiness? with names.
Which way did the wind point that morning did he listen.
Keen and able and wet was the stone.

215.

What was the stone's name your honor we need to tell.
Travertine or gneiss schist or circumstance.
Everything we see is evidence of that crime.
We read the world backwards and wrote it down.
Unship your mastwork and bend the Bible back.
I know there's a lover hidden in the salt.

216.
And from the cloud her voice rejoins me.
Broken like sea beasts I weltered partial on the strand.
And foreign people walked among my bones.
O lick yourself together and stand up she said.
I stood like Christian hungry for authority.
My mutinous bones came to their senses from her voice.

217.
Hexagon my beehive my little room of rooms.
Be solid like the wax lost when the bronze is cast.
Airy perennial like those flowers made of cloud.
I read them once in a book I had to write.
And there you are caparisoned with living breath.
Lasting no longer than a Pentecost of minds.

218.
Of course I mean you who else have you ever been.
The pewter sky Iago's sneers unheard.
Trust nothing I can't touch the leper said.
An island is the furthest thing from sea.
The invisible kingdom speaks all night as waves.
I hear memory dismembers the mind.

219.
Lost at sea the eye recalculates the heart.
I am alone the owner of all distances.
The sky turns into a flock of birds and feeds me.
Their wings' unruliness wakes up the wind.
A sack of sand to bring the sea back home.
Null irrigation paddies pure rice your mind.

220.

I do this for the eyes of women with which all men read.
Soon it will be time for now it hurts.
The monster of Capital can't help itself nobody home inside.
Every vote sends men to war.
How can you be tired of what I haven't said.
This massive fugue escapes from no one.

221.

Leave the heroics for Sunday go to church.
Say your prayers make your own meanings in the words

you say.

Moths were made to serve the candle flame.
I am clumsy with eternity.
Now I stare across the sea and read.
The white cliffs of never.

222.

Live simple on the edge of yourself.
Make an arrow won't miss the heart takes thirty years.
Its point so keen it opens wide but does not kill.
I found a trace of her beneath the hill.
Followed her footsteps till I caught fire.
Things are allowed to follow one another.

223.
The way the sky is always letting go.
Truth is geography the shortest line between here and you.
Close the book and open up the names.
A name is a bell that tolls true in your head.
Ignore the specious identities of men and listen.
Once a door is closed it never opens.

224.
I put everything in this little bowl it all fits in.
Will anybody ever really fill the cup.
How big a car is yet it goes I think.
Let me hug you from behind so I see the things you see.
Nature has no nature of its own.
Blood rhymes with madness rhymes with glow.

225.
Rhyme tells us nothing but does make us doubt.
Gifted raptors glide along the mind.
Dried mud remembers what the water said.
Ask forgiveness of each thing before they sleep.
When you're the only one awake you're most asleep.
Hume's golden mountain believe anything but your eyes.

226.
Half an hour into judgment Jericho.
We named our roads from books we don't believe.
But language is the purest contradiction.
Lights on an island that isn't there.
Help me to know beyond beyond and no believing.
When you get there it's somewhere else.

227.
Learning a new language growing new teeth.
I'm diggin' to girling? Sure, be ye gone.
We hear what we want to hear ears stuffed with resemblance.
But she walked across the patio in moonlight.
Down that staircase wide enough for rain.
A substrate people with time in their mouths.

228.
A word changes in the water of your mouth be afraid.
She lived in the gap between a thing and its name.
Late again for early Mass as any lover.
Kept his whole religion in his head.
Swift in rapid currents a slim idea.
She cuts old battle from his gore-stained hair.

229.
It doesn't stand it just keeps listening.
Sun works its old phlebotomy on the clouds.
The strongest are the ones who run away.
We beat the Romans and kept our gods Westphalia.
Design is round but meaning's cubical.
The last days live inside us in their majesty.

230.
Of course a Gnostic what else could an iris be.
Shattered by the sight of what we want to see.
At their desks they pray to money to give them God.
Who can believe outside his hands.
Twelve years old again new pen before puberty.
Fimbul-winter things come too soon.

231.
Of all the languages which one is best.
Your tongue in my mouth speaking.
Inhaled the smile from the lover's face.
People in a park at play one kneeling.
Breath exchange rescue from old prana.
In the school of Himerology excavate the mind.

232.
Pale not too committed tentative green spring.
Still the elm remembers she was Eve she was E.
Overgrown sea thick with trees of air.
So many Athenians died here their bones are flutes.
Behavior of sound waves under water.
Life is a shadow on grass he said we asked What is grass.

233.
Meeting at the glad shampoo the smell of young.
Because we were sunshine to each other and wet sand.
Always a different island has no more to say.
Make it simple like a bride to be.
A bridge to night a tree with no comparisons.
Ecphrasis is *speaking from* what I see sees me.

234.
Who are you who punish crime with crime.
Elderberry statesmen of the world soursweet be good for you.
Six of us always here waiting for six others.
Sight of a girl just standing there a hex galore.
Mourning for the dead sift sand from your shoes.
We mourn those most we didn't know at all.

235.
Addled elm the wind a poplar tunnel to aspen ocean.
A man suntanned from too much shade.
Last week's storms did not disturb the sea.
Reach into the distances to become yourself.
A sum a song is what the right hand said.
Counting mere increase as melody America.

236.
Dare temple to rebuild in our day.
But temple is patriarch and Rome is revenge.
Interminable history of getting and getting it wrong.
Progress is a child asleep in a typhoon.
Nor'easter now the trees know can dance a psalm.
The history of the world is one short sentence.

237.
These sums I sweated from who knows how many.
A question mark is part of the disease.
Everyone has to do it but why me.
I have never been part of everyone why now.
My lowly station is my arrant pride.
How do you say No in Yessish.

238.
Language is flirtation.
I would the air the air's enough and Donizetti.
Cloudy sea doves lumber towards their seed.
O the sideswipe of the drifting gull utter her control.
Invent another animal to be a kind of number.
A wheel takes you as far as you can see.

239.
I have no gleam of emptiness in me the raja's stone.
Woke inside a word a cough a storm at sea.
A kiss might have whistled the wind up.
The woods sleep the dream of the uninvited guest.
Lonely work beneath the sea to map lost cities.
The blonde surveyor lunches on the rocks.

240.
We had to bake the bread he made the miracle.
Learn to talk is find a place to stand.
The supernatural inherits from the natural.
Wild carrot in the parson's field or is it mandrake.
We settle for the real when we could have the dream.
I gave you all the meaning I had left.

241.
"Look at the" sea "and remember."
Insurmountable evidence in your hand or your hand.
To make your mind into your will is how the soul becomes.
Taste me next time always by the love-house door.
Keep your dearest promises from far away.
We are crucified on each other.

242.
Be there when I wake is all I wake for thee.
Strange collaborations called from the air.
Island when you watch the sunrise your work is done.
Saying their prayers is putting on tight clothes.
We use so little muscle of what we own.
I'm saying all this just because I'm you.

243.
Never forget the one in the front row that's why you're here.
We do this for others because we have no selves.
The wind so fierce why makes me happy.
No heave of sail just implicit destinations.
The dangerous voyage of being here.
Clutching an eraser your fingers tremble.

244.
No time for living in a quiet life.
I grab you by the adjective and rip it off.
Fill the plastic pail with sea and drink it home.
We are angels at each other too.
Fisherman fisherman don't haul the wrong catch.
We are scared of each other armed only with shtick.

245.
A little book you carry in your hand.
The book doesn't know who reads it.
It remembers everything but your hands your eyes.
To *Makiawisug* fairies of our local hill offer maize.
They were here before the moon.
All love is provisional but theirs.

246.
Heavy heart of a star a stone green as money.
We see its light refracted as the sea.
Moshup waded the middle sea up to his knees.
Heaped up stones the way children archipelago.
She sat in the water till she became the land.
My hand flat on the small of your back.

247.
Or too many lost to have a simple road.
The inner arrow shows the fish to go.
The weathercock also knows the latest news.
She worked her sorrows in between the words.
We touch the wall to prove that we exist.
There was a temple now there is just us.

248.
Be enough to the stars and swallow the sea.
Everything is trying to be me.
Scraps of meat still fresh on a dead man's plate.
The classroom cracks open like an orange.
Overripe children pass scriptures in the dark.
When I was a child my wall a luminous crucifix.

249.
By the landlock by the look of him.
I love thee stranger woman in the prim apart.
Ceaseless scordatura on the heartstrings taut.
We are related solely by language love.
Our language lets our bodies touch.
Language fucks us both the same.

250.
We need exact description Granville Wilkins.
No more comparisons essences alone.
I love you for your outstretched couch.
There is not much me in what I say.
Deliver the moony balcony from family houses.
I was so stupid when I am young.

251.
Hexes in the wood Roman march a thousand steps.
The witches watch the troops mile by.
The murmur of their minds becomes the wind the resin of the
wood retains.
Could the feather lift the bird or when.
It was *remorse* drove Juan to the always next.
The law is grass under no one's feet.

252.
This is how they'll speak a hundred years.
Three graces grouped inside her single mirror.
A million ghosts in every moment throng.
Elbow my way through clamorous identities.
How many days bare blue desire.
To hurt to heal see no one's there.

253.
In the Cornmarket selling explanations.
Is there any sense before you make it.
I hate suspense this hour's the appointed time.
She can feel his mind all over her.
Sea spray I mourn the things I made you lose.
Listen to the sea upbraid the shore.

254.
Moshup he brought the ocean back from the moon.
I blame myself for all I didn't know.
That child is back with his bright pail.
Experiment try living solely on nutritious light.
Lunar-power machinery of desire.
Sap rises no surprises.

255.
The order in which things come to mind itself is matter.
Rip the bandage off the sky at last.
See the nature of the primal wound.
Have lived in the between so long old friend.
But in crystal hillside they build me in their story.
I belong to their images a quiet woman far away.

256.
Cast off resemblances fill encyclopedias.
The broken radio emits a broken song.
There is much to be said for adolescence.
When the green lion roars by the virgin's gazebo.
Open the door the room is full of rain.
The words are wooden blocks we their sinister children.

257.
Granite slabs float through the lower air.
The old face who saw me from the rock.
I mourn your fall your profile fills me still.
He spoke inside and told me how to be.
Dig up some grain from before any war.
Grind your grain to words both fine and coarse.

258.
Can I listen long enough to hear a single word.
Time splice and northern ruin King of Thule.
How can one desire what is not given.
Broken irises in the rain don't try to limit beauty.
Courier of Evening read enough to learn the marshes.
Shadow of someone on cattails in the tidal flats.

259.
Slow the deeps of ink the word unwritten shows.
None of this is easy though it seems so.
Lucid intervals like falling down the stairs.
Often enough to see the obvious he said.
So many from have turned away solve for any me.
I wanted and she wouldn't what kind of isle is that.

260.
Drive father's car deep into mother's woods.
Poor Romeo roses not reeds on the near shore.
A girl who went to Eden and never wrote home.
A million ways to interrupt one dream.
Spintrian postures of the heavenly cadets.
Push the animal of mind into the starting gate.

261.
Quilted sky suits this old house earth that lives us.
A woman in the clutch of music asks for pain.
I'll pay you for the touch of your skin the coin of mine.
Wait by the toll bridge to Cochecton it's only years.
Bring down your hammers lightly on the Delaware.
I was here before you were and lit the lamp above.

262.
The stone the builders rejected has become the bird in
                                                the wind.

The heart wants to know so slow.
Why put the wind near me if it were not for mine.
Eat another grammar from the food you buy.
Because there is so much so desire.
A parked car speeds through another golden gate.

263.
Never fail the beacon on the hilltop the voice.
Seared in the flame of seeing.
The Old Masters knew when to look away.
Long ago shattered all the mirrors.
Sky is a mirror shows everything but me.
He unpacks the cloud he nails the wind to an oak tree.

264.
Dare the soprano's green air to ride the blue wheel.
Time called this morning and I answered.
Passageway between the stones my feet too wide.
Big egret fishing in shoals a wary eye on me.
But that was yesterday and this is even further back.
Not caring much in memory but on its knees.

265.
Birds keep wanting to be said.
Connection is the riskiest thrill skydiving in the heart.
And now the birds are feeding from her lap.
Light broken on the bay Viking longboats glide.
Through the grill of speech we prisoners converse.
We are the walls around our prison.

266.
The soul's a breed of blackbird flies away.
Only my old shoes know where I've been.
Have I gone against my grain and stood when I would run.
Question the question and you'll see for miles.
This is what it's like for you when I'll be dead.
You can even call it by my name and it will speak.

267.
Mute difference between man and rock.
How can there be so many languages I'm missing something.
Human like you I should understand no matter what you say.
A branch of pomegranate broken off the fruit still on.
Sink your head in your lap and remember.
Old brick factories on the river the heart fluttering.

268.
For once the rhythm breathes but not of breath.
You never tell me what you're looking at.
Witangemot where senators talk clouds into the sky.
My fervor waits the absolute her voice on the stupid phone.
Listen you who'll be twice Lord Mayor of nowhere.
Day of glad clouding in the synagogue of rain.

269.
All my old verses are right the rhymes are wrong.
Truth is always the other way.
Spinsters in sunlight the fugue begins anew.
Crosswise crabby like a dead man's tune.
Of course the dead are speaking what else is the wind.
History is what slips between the fingers.

270.
The old have cute interns to help them die.
Experience is a leaky vessel founders as my life.
"Look at the" clouds "and remember," he said.
Can one have so much there's none to throw away.
Resumptions of spiritual discipline a tree in wind.
What kind of tree and of what wood is spirit made.

271.
Clear and woolly at once a bright idea in too soon a mind.
Tall pine forest on the way to Callicoon my mind began.
Matter is madera is material is mother now who are you.
How stupefied I was a child amazed at everything out loud.
A fingerprint is a map of the island see where the little hill.
Look look I cried I can't see without saying.

272.
Princes rescue maidens are savage flames.
You have hero to get through hedge of your own heart.
The ones who talk to me from clouds are clouds.
Everlastedly everchangingly emissaries of.
Entropy applies only to systems: do not be a system.
The whole law standing on one foot.

273.

Asking sunshine for its middle name.

You don't even know my mothers are.

A hero is a heap of stones some scholar said.

No chance beyond the moon the old map shows.

This secret map I found shows time.

Finds the entrances to times that are not now.

274.

No way to know if past or future shown.

There are bright horsemen and brave machines.

All I can say is that whatever's true is *then*.

Then is the land undiffered and unlawed.

Then quiet people move deeply among their lives.

Then is a set of musics half familiar half of brass.

275.

Rabbit under bush man in the street scary how everything fits.

They look out from themselves and saw and sang.

What else can a blackbird or a pilgrim do.

Forgive the stars your long disaster.

Voices scribe grooves in each material.

I playback Eve when I fondle wood.

276.

Please remember it's a fugue how could it end.

Stories have no end we'll still be looking.

The loose ends are what we live by.

Don't give me theory they have no morals.

Your politics a shadow of your bank account.

Slaves at the mercy of slaves but we sing.

277.
Into the time map slipped your fingers spread.
That country just like ours but no one slays.
Only Death there is allowed to kill and no one knows.
It's just like us but we are not.
It's just like us but they remember.
You catch a glimpse of it across bodies of water.

278.
Meager as it is utopia by abstentions known.
We need it there to wipe our greasy lips.
I want to make the language of to come.
A fugue does what you have to follow.
The more you rub it the sooner done.
Time to consult the oracle open up your shirt.

279.
No narrative nothing happens we're still here.
The sea is good for fine distinctions.
Bronze spear-head footstep in the sand.
Six seals murdered on Nantucket the reef like teeth.
The face of the sea is the mind at rest.
She never left and she'll never come back.

280.
Things you see before the others wake.
Who is it when the morning reddens.
I am sure of where I thought I went.
I saw I was a little mouse below her chair.
Egypt heart out of body alabaster still on fire.
Not light but a slow erasure of the dark.

281.
Rub away the writing to see what it said.
What is seen in dawn its deer.
For every hour hath its Fauna sure.
They live among us we hardly ever see.
Whatever their name is we call them good.
That's what morning means I'm for all of you.

282.
Hidden symmetries sea glow under dawn glow.
Over luminous sea a light is sacrilege.
Even a candle shows too much.
Gather the remnants of the defeated dark.
The dark is what you need the bones of understanding.
Resistance resistance tall walking in the wind.

283.
The light behind the ordinary mind.
There are things dawn shows day takes away.
Now light enough to see nothing there.
The ambiguities mean us from before the grave.
Once rhyme is gone the music of the mind.
Two hundred years little by little the song ascending.

284.
We dream from magma do kisses come from cloud.
We are betweeners in between.
And then he said *Love lives only on the stairs.*
He was there before me they turn to meet us.
The red of what will happen meets the green of was.
Every idea is a bad idea.

285.
I hear a windstorm in the sun itself.
What he called angels were even stranger guests.
What comes to mind's often sacred script.
Ahimsa's where it starts harm nobody at all.
Help all you can and know your mind.
Artemis drew close to give me comfort.

286.
When I forgive all men the world's reborn.
Shut up and let me worship thee he thought.
This is wrong this is mere thinking.
Be small and hide in shadows.
I borrowed his mustache and never gave it back.
Pages are dense with imaginary meanings.

287.
Renew the forest the stories will keep coming.
The whole thing is mostly ocean mostly waiting.
I thought the dragon was a bird inside.
The burning star behind your ribs.
Rete mirabile the way up is the way down.
The angel pointed upward and watched us fall.

288.
The sameness of the midday sea mothers fine distinctions.
Mel dat rosa apibus one neuter and two feminines a hint.
In the ancient lab white rats are sleeping.
I tied a stream of water to a string of air and saw.
Red powder swallowed every dawn a month of moons.
Now I am old and sleek and durable as stone.

289.
Each person runs inside a different cache of elements.
My Christmas chemistry set basement logwood waterglass.
Make ink from memory and write tomorrow.
Do my feet reach to the ground yet.
Gum of peach tree sticky from the world outside.
The eerie light that comes from looking.

290.
Why was it I couldn't find the farm.
I walked all over London looking for me.
I thought my home would have my shadow in it.
Silent as wolves on a moonless hill.
Raspberry bushes leggy thorned all in white flower.
They were beside you when you found the dark sea.

291.
Quisling weather to match the heart's decrees.
I want it to be new so light begins.
On this shift a co-worker of the obvious.
A child like all the rest of now.
The sea so calm I need a shave.
No reason to say anything but you.

292.
The unfathomable pronoun.
The empty bag of tricks.
The dog at the larder whimpering.
The pine tree rife with finches.
The footnote's tedious fascination.
The almost suicide at Marble Hill.

293.
Nobody blues their bedsheets anymore.
Children we are of wafture and of reeds.
Small dismal evangelists chirp nearby.
The bundles of Purkinje the marvelous net.
Careworn crusaders trapped in a book.
That day I stopped drinking.

294.
Then I looked at the river my back to Spuyten Duyvil.
I don't have to feel like this.
I don't have to feel.
Poetry leaves all the connections to you.
Not a river the Harlem Ship Canal.
My whole life to learn to write this line.

295.
Spider in the classroom droits de l'homme.
Subject means topic means agent ego means thrall.
Words change their valance while you sleep.
Lovers at the gaunt assizes.
The word means you to think it.
Your mind on softest down behind her ear you whisper.

296.
Now the orbit of the moon is straight now it is never.
I want to claim how full your slim face is with hearing.
Wake up before the birds and no one groaning.
Implicit intercourse in far-off gardens.
From shrubbery the lute twangs utter.
You hear it all as foreign language.

297.
What could be further than song.
Rise into cloud unred the warning tide.
Nowhere near the middle of the mind.
Mood be more as our might littles.
Exasperate cross-borne conquistadors.
Hoist your language in high poetry.

298.
From ash and beast-fat boil a cleaning.
The war is over come back home.
Guano from the walls of heaven heal our soil.
Pantomime Bible in which a real Ruth grieves.
Noah took only the misfits on his ark.
The old beasts never soiled their speech by speaking.

299.
Pure animals are yet to come and they will speak.
We will no longer think that we're alone.
Nothing is as or other than it seems.
Others he revises himself he can't revise.
If I trusted you more I would wake up now.
A satin slip conceals my politics.

300.
A day describes the world as far as sleep.
Needy consciousness makes fools of thinking men.
They do not know how who what they know.
Everything they think they know is lies.
Only conscious fiction can hint at truth.
Heart thinks you're sleeping in its other room.

301.

Wing sung over horizon here heard hard.
Not so much a mist as a vagueness rising.
But the Tuscan argued vague means beautiful.
The sun spurts images to earth Egyptians knew.
Everything was bright enough to be.
A few dreams left before we come to now.

302.

In the heart of the green man.
To carry herself into the woods and then.
It was too much like what he wanted to.
My id is another country who is speaking.
Sometimes just don't want to see.
Bronze mirror glows inside the ground.

303.

Seeing they say is bad for the eyes.
How far the mouth can kiss.
There are more elements than animals they'll find.
Chemistry is a halfway house.
It all is folklore done with funny numbers.
Believe nothing and love everything c'est tout.

304.

Belief wrecks the balance boat capsizes.
Belief unhinges fleshly certainties.
She is the May Pole all by herself.
The agèd poet is younger than you.
Challenge the great on their own ground.
You've got to be at least Caravaggio.

305.
Staircase to Parnassus still means a fugue.
A fugue on if you see be and only fugues have heart.
We all are fugitives hurry to no one home.
Addiction polite word for selfishness.
Store-bought wise doom burn this book.
Nowheres near the middle of the mind.

306.
They call them people they live in sun.
Myriad myriads one mother of God.
Follow the sea long enough come to a self.
But is it yours the pilot roared.
I am ashamed of what I think I see.
Haven't you been given hints enough to feel your skin.

307.
Read all the words that aren't written.
Literature is built of beautiful denials.
Don't be clever just be cute like rain.
New let the wind shampoo your hair.
Let the sea be my bedtime story never stops.
I accuse myself of listening stole you with my ears.

308.
Ideals are murderers let loose when men are sleeping.
Don't you love how things just are a praise of Venus.
They have ideas but no idea.
The 'soul in judgment' on the cliffs of more.
I can't know what I mean till I see what it says.
Write it down and turn your back like duellists pacing off.

309.
Grassy mind perplexed without desires.
The premise is a mind as such beyond the brain.
Take off your wings and walk like a Christian.
Can you land on my life little bird.
Sea same as sky the ground is always floating.
Things you never bothered thinking.

310.
A thought crossing my mind no more mine than a bird
                                                    crossing the sky.
We belong to what we think not the other way round.
Philosophers are noisy victims of what they thought.
Revising sunlight so it's thicker than Provence.
That's not what I mean I only wanted something to eat.
Tame wolves are waiting till you sleep to eat your dream.

311.
There is a truth two bodies know that sex undoes.
Knowing without doing is the highest human right.
Leave me alone with you a little while.
Doing is an anxious substitute for being.
No one knows the mind like me.
Sometimes we go back to brain and start again.

312.
Herm herm a head without a thing.
Patient Alcibiades destroys the state.
State is a cop with his pocket full of us.
Handcuffs glitter in stagey sunshine.
We build things to show to foreigners.
We keep our natives in the dark.

313.
A true anarchist would slay his ego the first tyrant.
Where does your self come from my fine fish.
Blue from the smokehouse party on the hill.
Quiet the miracles let architecture do its social work.
Glass walls for a library make us read in civic context.
If I can't be a dancer I'll build cathedrals.

314.
Dancers use the wrong parts of themselves.
Be close enough dance with the smell of your breath.
Only tangent bodies dance the dance is not for eyes.
Touch is a profanation of some unknown thing.
The radical intellect must dispense with meaning.
No park benches on the moon.

315.
The reverse happens all the time or tree.
She saw them sitting there three moons and no weather.
She bore the crowns from all of them and put one on.
Come back to me when you know who you are.
I will always tell you otherwise no lies.
We slept inside the little glimpse of skin no war.

316.
Don't think of all that think just of this.
Every monosyllable wants to be the moon.
A paradise of particulars and the sea.
Hatchet hack some dead tree back to life.
Where were the ripe figs when he needed.
Come back and be my daughter after all.

317.
This is getting personal benches looking for their park.
Trees are always hiding something isn't it.
Raw wood my dearest treasure ever whose.
A wren in judgment midsummer nears.
He saw clearly the two gods of that valley.
It is our duty to nourish local deity.

318.
Sometimes the dream police come too late to revise the night.
The thing you love in her is everywhere.
Then the sinners came and sealed the sea.
Love is the physics of difference metaphysics of hope.
Sun glare on the sea stop dreaming alone.
Dream-linked sleepers rule the world isn't that some novel.

319.
Sometimes only sameness says me.
We have what we can't have.
Hard stone stairs of Irish towers hide in hearts.
No one awake but the sea and it's snoring.
Light-hearted lies like a lily.
All he wanted from you was your youth you'll lose anyway.

320.
Put things down till your hands are empty.
When reality starts up again try to be missing.
It annoys you to be told what to do don't I.
But where else are all the fish to live.
Plucking the ripest morning clears his throat.
Fishing boats in the sun glare untie the knot.

321.
We linger lately not a boulder hide behind us.
Treaty with the sound handshake with the ocean.
If I disagree with you enough you'll love me.
I am a dissident with no despot but myself.
I can't get enough of not being me.
I take a staircase everyday a drug called waking.

322.
Not by impulse but by increment.
If you can't make love to god who can you to.
Welcome the other other boat the one comes in.
From a bullfrog's mouth an answer comes if ask.
Learning to speak quiet becomes a stone.
Sly diphthongs of rational discourse.

323.
The whole island's going to a wedding.
I don't want to belong I want to be long.
Birds are naturally Jewish.
Monkeys are secular humanists.
Too many weddings too few marriages.
The bigger the wedding the shorter the marriage.

324.
Wind brings news from wild roses on the rocks.
The serpent is the sea itself that rings us round.
Under the ruined abbey crypts full of news.
I hide inside your sense of me.
Was one more waiting or was it leaf alone.
The son of man nowhere to lay his head.

325.
Without my glasses I could see one star.
How bright that means or close it spoke me.
Tho-rangs the trough of meaning just before light.
If you perceive are you awake or is the light inside instead.
Now I declare the one I love is north it all comes down.
They talk about liberty but all they mean is talk.

326.
Let the perceivers perceive the whistles blow.
The wrong-armed Scythians breathe Attic calm.
Make me a soldier mother make me a god,
All you can ever be is what you wonderful are.
They carry money in the afterlife their images.
A good novel is one you don't have to finish reading.

327.
Liberty of a silent man my father's potency.
Freedom is silence.
Make trouble or make art leave war and love alone.
Consider Achilles with blueblack hair sprawled in the dust.
Consider the pure alternative to anything.
Consider the financial affairs of the long-time dead.

328.
Every death is suicide the wise man said.
Suicide is just one more disease the wise man said.
We have free will we can go on living the wise man said.
We know nothing but what happens and there is no truth.
Death is always waiting for our assent.
In the army of the dead we'll serve our term.

329.
Then come again and be my horoscope strange star.
Strange is stranger from another strand a foreigner a god.
There are ambitions deadlier than cyanide.
Know the worst and hurry through the gate.
Lurk in folklore like a child in the bath.
The man thinks the dog barks.

330.
Any garden is where the gnomes can wait.
Matter is the product of interpretation.
Reasoning and imagining are the same coin.
Walk with baby steps the alley of the id.
Engrave all tombstones with the resurrection date.
I like to pass a house where daylight shows right through.

331.
What does one sacrifice in writing this not waiting for that.
Every work of art haunted by the shadows of the unmade.
There'll always be another chance for now.
Fill your belly with surmises the feds will always lose.
Be about grasses instead be about stone.
They are close to permanent in your chronotome.

332.
They hunt you with light rays from invisible stars.
It's the daytime stars that persuade the ways you are.
Bend it around tomorrow tie it to yesterday.
Blue of the Day of Judgment belong to the color you are.
Everything always starts tomorrow.
Too many waiting for I to be.

333.
You tell them by their faces green algebra the sea.
The more complex the closer to truth.
Can you call it moral when leaves are on the elm.
The specific is always in disguise an impostor of the actual.
Whenever there is nakedness the balcony is quiet.
Queen Libuše delights in flute and harp K. 299.

334.
Near and far away at once like a fruit.
Still room for comparisons a girl climbing the hill.
Radio one time rapture sunburn in the ear.
Fire hydrant every navel of the earth.
She has so many bodies everywhere.
Time for men to start giving birth.

335.
Nothing at all inside the body.
The body is all out and outward bound.
I'm near the end of the beginning.
The wind englobes me it all is listening.
Show what you're made of before you leave the room.
The body is hollow and what did you learn.

336.
Bell-6 bongs at the channel mouth a wind word heard.
We hear fence we think wood they think what wood closes in.
Old tune our town.
Loveliness only in the stains.
Goldfinches come from the woods primitive accumulation.
Who listens to the Ladies listening.

337.
All the Fates do is give us back our words as things.
Our only business is to praise I think.
Organ-grinder with Darwin on a leash the Rights of Beast.
Well-nigh forgotten how to do the human talk.
Among the hydrangeas though some blue is happening.
We are the silent parts of music made us.

338.
From tacit cart survey a calmed sea.
I have nothing greater than to be.
Things work well when we're off dreaming.
India again last night no exit visa.
Ambient light controls the speed of thought.
She spreads her legs and there are hands instead.

339.

She lay asleep and there was one rose.
Our chalices encourage such shy bees.
Gloom-sunk drinkers at green tables.
A credit card to ease the bolt back.
Art's a manx cat with naught to follow.
The farmer looks out despairing at the frost.

340.

Don't you see we come from a different earth.
We want to go back to that clean place.
Pure topology and one poplar tree.
Streets run from us and scroll up as we pass.
Where we go is light and where we turn is text.
No toothache and no tetanus all languages are one.

341.

Always another customer waiting for some meat.
He sails by mouth across the choppy bay.
Seals sun on the rocks he waves to his mothers.
Men perish avoiding the obvious.
Sentenced to the sentence one speaks.
Nothing moves that fast.

342.

Couldn't we make just one mistake together.
A monster but a monster sleeps.
I fear my mind's on something else.
Another argument goes on unheard unheeded.
Try to see in the window so much light.
Puffed-out baby sparrow beak up to be fed.

343.
Did I wake up before I did.
Is all of it just sunlight on the sea.
Who are you to renew this inquiry.
In Academe they sell the truth but never tell it.
Slope of the ridge-pole age of the house a gull.
Elegant is grackle in sunlight till it speaks.

344.
Lacking a self we envy others selves we think they have.
Can anything be shorter than this.
Ask a bird and a tree will answer.
Sleepy sunlight closes visionary deals.
The clock names names the skin tells time.
When I was small green hedges were my friends.

345.
No statement is all wrong except this.
Live for truth or lose it to yourself.
Spillways of the skin let excess feeling out.
How young I was when I was young.
The light seems very far away today.
Urgency in afterglow what does dark demand.

346.
All these uncarved inscriptions from no rock.
Save the tale it must tell on the earth is waiting.
I walked into the vein of quartz led down inside me.
Misremembered elegances from an empire ago.
Prompt to disbelieve in what they most required.
Far away a rainbow stricken on the sea.

347.
Kiss the log that lets the story swim to safety.
Romance is salt love loves the woods.
Deep in the glass mountain conspirators analyze.
I am folklore you are city.
Walls around the feelings make sense of fences.
Every else has a somewhere of its own.

348.
Of course it might all be wrong the epitaph.
Season ticket to the fall of man.
Confederate money common in my youth.
Wayward testimonials to a girl gone again.
A park condemned to death all night.
Yearning for the sound of distant cities.

349.
A denser text to lay before the company.
I put out what it says the rest is you.
This too is written in a foreign language.
Language is mist on the sea language is morning.
Stay alchemist till the white turns blue.
Farewell text dwell handsome in the clemencies.

350.
Weight-bearing in the wonder world a hand a house.
Gods go on vacation in celebrities be kind to them.
Nothing is easy if it loves you.
When the god is gone she mumbles pointless on the stage.
Don't mistake this for imperative.
Secret answers to the ten commandments.

351.
Mortgage value of unoccupied ideas.
A premise is a wilderness of guess.
Why are there deities in the morning.
Near enough to judgment a crow decides.
Try to touch the other side of this try to milk the now.
Night is an anchor tangled deep in weed.

352.
Shielded from brightness able to see.
The Temple will never be rebuilt it's here all round us.
There is some forever in little things.
I write against the seneschals of thought the idolmakers.
To keep language safe for the trivial the uncommodity
                                    the gods.
Did you really think I am an animal and which.

353.
This endish feeling when daylight comes that bright vampire.
Disco ball twirling over sea horizon.
And this is for you just a tap on the wrist.
Quiet enough to hear a sparrow touch down one just did.
Rivalrous islands homeopathy of space.
Cure birds by birds cure words by words.

354.
Take the sea back home with me.
The whole ocean fits inside the hollow moon.
Where did water come from.
The jabber of the gods in everything.
In silence nothing can be understood.
Words fierce and blank as colors are.

355.
The birds know something I don't know.
Subway empathy faces in the roar of sound.
Someday they may write with me again.
Only let the words decide.
This harsh practice that rules my life.
I dreamed these words they must be true.

356.
It moves also through air the ghost of water.
Lax narration impeaches family sagabank.
Say say all around and you say mercy mercy.
Grim arrangements who knows what lost days.
Does rain rheum ravish knees.
I met them both when I was new and he's the best.

357.
White German shepherd ghost of a wolf.
Simplicity of puberty in pale churches.
Shrapnel deadly from previous ideas.
Don't think that thought again by water vow.
Philosophy bred in mountains dies in town comes back by sea.
The sea thinks nothing.

358.
What will show its head above the waves today.
But I want the secret parts of what you think.
The humid thought below the conscious island.
Will I be mainland and no enemies.
Count by bells not clock you're free of time.
I will not go back again but which way is back.

359.
The whole sea is one single secret.
I have withdrawn a cloud hid my voice.
Zanies on a hollow stage echo of their prattle.
Far away the sea tries to tell a shell how to respond.
Say something to the wolf its fangs will understand.
Blue o Christ cathedrals under the sea.

360.
The cost of being.
Going home is the best vacation.
Do the starlings still stir beneath the eaves.
Why is everything new again.
Marvel on the roads the long green riff.
Here the air stands still and waits for your next move.

361.
Walk outside and understand again.
Leaf-scar on the twig of time has its story too.
I see a child and feel the mother's pain.
So long to be born to bear to give birth.
And in the twinkling on an eye another decides.
Sprawled on tidal shingle somebody has to care.

362.
Petroglyphs of waking.
Find myself a mesolith again.
The court rules against itself and vanishes.
The Mystery of the Virtuous Police.
Ambling even now towards innocence.
Squalid motorcar parked beside the shrine.

363.
Devious lucidity a mind on the make.
Alone to ask the mother to receive.
Of all the things a bird to say.
Childless couples dance beneath the hill.
Vast emergence of human feeling hoof on the heart.
Decoding Baltic grammars whence all human poetry.

364.
There's too much here to find anything.
Bluemaker's cross meant a different agony.
They all are real and I am not or just romantic music.
Measure the frictional interface and feel her.
Something like home but further away.
Sometimes these are analects but sometimes true.

365.
I want to wait outside and blossom through the gate.
And if his father chanced to look down as he hung there.
And if the passing traffic were going anywhere.
Breeze makes us remember what never happened.
Something dear enough to need by listening.
The god departs the singer crumples to the stage.

366.
Walking on the underside of other or walk on water.
He pulled the tune's strings now all the tones are pure apart.
Song is the shadow of desire.
Close to judgment day a mile away.
From here you see the fringes of his tallith swing.
If only actors had no names at all.

367.
Who comes is a yachtsman every morning.
The river mouth and no one listening.
The Indian names we mispronounce control our lives.
Environmental apathists use me up and wait for more.
It *has* to be more complex than we think.
Waiting outside a bookstore in falling snow.

368.
Soon let the water flow back in isn't it time for music.
To have amassed all this experience and still want.
Don't want water uphill just want August snow.
Settle for the most improbable every time.
A far cry from being natural.
An island's built of silences and light.

369.
I'll come in my true form and visit your dream.
Don't think the man you see when you see me.
I keep saying listen but I never say to what.
It isn't me it isn't music it's probably the dining room table.
They play pinochle they read the future they eat lamb.
Hear me lucid incoherence of Henry James's last day.

370.
Wet shale the color of its ancient mud astonished mainland.
Elegant arbitrage a bluefish smoked on shore.
Apt to order a sluggish miracle or two despite.
The journey of which you speak vanished long ago in sea.
Wherever I touch the walls of it are wet.
You are horizon but which one is you.

371.
Approximate evidence rim of the sun.
A mystery to come between you and the inner temple.
The size of going is somewhere else.
We were walking down Holborn once again.
The years didn't forget that much of me.
Dream ballast the moon looks cellulite.

372.
The measurement of the face measures me.
No god I am but seem to seem.
Velvet revers on threadbare astrakhan.
Humans wear collars to prove they know not what.
I strike the board and cry my way abroad.
The ancient dignity of protestant.

373.
Leave the loss to other milkings.
Cruelty is built into the system the Sir gets all.
In direst calamity interest keeps accruing.
Soul in dormancy poems collect stray heartbeats.
Meters and measures the Tongue Tower in Thonon.
Speak your native language just for once.

374.
If you have a language if there is.
For you the smelters strive in Minnesota.
Arbalest handshakes I am dangerous to know.
I come to you with all my sheep arrayed.
Poetry stinks of human feelings reminiscing.
Cloth of madness waited for you at the airport.

375.
You waved to me from a window was no house.
Interpreting vedanta by high school trig.
I think I am a school of angry rabbis preaching.
I wake thrilled by Nietzsche's great authentic voice.
From a man's book we inherit his body in our own.
The mountain climbed down his arteries into our veins.

376.
I have many gods but only one me.
Day off so much not to do.
Wending west among swans no lagoon.
No roads in New England run west or only one one.
Only the sun knows that way it's death to follow.
I thought you were in love with me but I never left the sea.

377.
Say it till the tiger lilies roar by the scholar's kitchen window.
Then say some more whatever you find to say.
This instruction goes on forever think river think weather.
Check the mail to see who slipped inside your mind.
All the things that I forgot come at me now.
Build a fortress in midair to hide in sheer transparency.

378.
Apologize for linking spirit knows you best.
In the cheese farm strange clean machines.
What do worms do with the lust Schiller gave them.
Ridiculous rhyme schemes evade the heart.
Cold-hearted pricks bookland politics.
Smile if it won't Saturday all the time.

379.
Crow call I must be home and maybe me.
Rain in the night there must be weather still.
Proof is like striptease you pretend you really care.
Or did she mean real solutions to imaginary problems.
I have to learn the grammar crows disclose.
Ruined brick house way back in the woods.

380.
Now I've forgotten how to turn the daylight on.
The cost of a paradox is measured in reputations.
The union forever of chemical innocence.
A committee of dragons and wolves can choose.
I keep demanding more of matter.
If you take one away not so much lost like trees in woods.

381.
Clus and *clar* turn by turn I don't know whom I serve.
If it sang from a different throat would we listen.
Mud-baths of sly potency quick you catch fire.
The sea I study now is green and tall.
I want to use only the simplest words.
When you look carefully at green all colors are there.

382.
Everything I am is a small part of you.
Thousands of mouths speaking one line each my epic.
I am with Merlin underground staring up her sky.
I don't understand me either but still it moves.
Sunlight suddenly a shadow says.
Thousands of them taking part in me.

383.
Aion the cerebrospinal fluid your knees also I have grasped.
I knelt before you to read the fine print of your skin.
Or does a man have to be his own encyclopedia.
Catch the sun for me and wise me up like it.
Make me useful to the rest of you like a piano.
Did I ever mean myself what he said.

384.
Partial to sunspots radio gets distracted from its music.
They call it static though it moves so fast.
The self is a fish he says but there is no sea.
All my livelong days to find an ocean.
Crows laugh and say you never found the land.
Come back and read me again when I grow up.

385.
Lantern-slides of the Holy Land aunts brought home.
She taught me woe the stones of Capernaum.
She explained the princes of the air Apollyon.
She read me stories no one wrote.
I understood mostly the smell of her old pretty clothes.
There is nothing inside the body it all just seems.

386.
It all is shine there is nothing but what seems.
Psalmless David shivered in his bed.
They brought him the thought of you to keep him warm.
You have slept with her too she is the girl next door.
The birds keep waking her from dreamless sleep.
Knock on her window to hear her speak.

387.
Weary of the seizing register the blonde assizes.
Now you know what the Bible means.
It's all part of the same conspiracy.
Listeners fraught with message yearn for quiet skin.
List all the things you hate and love them one by one.
Grass you green interference with our politics.

388.
All he ever wanted was to be somebody else.
Strange to have feelings at all the forest the shale.
Have you relented from religion yet or more.
Young trees thinking towards the sky.
Emergency birthright closet full of nos.
I'll touch you if you let me listen.

389.
If waiting is wanting what is being here.
Said fast enough it slips past sense and wakes.
Pale young hairs on my old arm but how.
Looking close sees everything again.
You cannot lose what you never heard.
Suns find gaps in foliage to bother through.

390.
Stendhal called the scrawny little Swiss a genius.
His music sounds like music and is maybe that enough.
If my hand is like a hand it can do what hands do.
If the word comes out of the mouth it finds its goal.
We're here all right but what can be done with us.
How do we make love across the Dardanelles.

391.
Thunder in the north the Mohawk drums of Claverack.
Summerlightning these things are meant to pass.
Weather is an immense reminder a Talmud of human time.
The way things work out or morning star.
The little left we need to leaf.
Sparrow-witted through thick air bespeaking.

392.
Write down the syllables we aren't speaking.
It might be the easier to be the other isn't it.
Sickbed see out on the river barges pass.
Spring with its tugboats and its mildewed sails.
We hide in the bottom of the boat.
Fingering the lady in her other life.

393.
But there is more to us than accusation.
Syllable tree seize fruit the sayable.
Terrible truth each one of us is the Incarnation.
We stake our claims between each breath.
Saying always makes it so.
The blind know the west wind by its smell.

394.
Could we only walk back before the covenant.
Go to the desert crazed by some idea.
In eighty volumes of Heidegger find what he said just for me.
And there the word was aflame on asphalt.
The winning horse keeps furthest from the rail.
Over white peonies hovered the specter of Roussel.

395.
I lead you through the obvious to the patent mystery.
All night the dead are coming up these stairs.
You can't think anything they haven't thought before.
All their fears are yours and furthest from the real.
Sometimes the dead are breathing that is me.
Only the things you say are ever different.

396.
How do we know a wind can a fugue tell us.
It makes the world go away isn't that enough.
They're all the same they all try to be flowers.
Come to the afterglow by sleight of hand.
The hidden teashop where language is created.
You thought the gods were ordinary girls.

397.
The real god is elsewhere hidden in what you say.
So many on their way to being me.
Truth in lying cars hurry to job.
Try to make it fit inside your spoon.
Whittling Oregon from a lump of peach gum.
You still can use what you can't do.

398.
Call them leaves they leave it up to you.
Dare not yield a single erg of what power you have.
Polecat policies in town halls mid-evening.
And there are animals also laying rain or shine play too.
Men ran with knives to slay the echoes of their voices.
No more *of* now a thing is on its own and knows.

399.
Let things be a walk or two away.
The longer you sleep the mother your skin.
Then you become river and they love you.
The moon is near compared to you.
Fugue on four voices I and you and she and we.
All the secrets tumble out now god knows.

400.
I live away from what I try to know.
Analytic language where a word is is what it says.
I lock you in the tower you lock me out in the woods.
I am terrified of all that is not me the wonder all round.
You let me in only when I'm far away.
The ancient language you milk into my ears.

401.
When you're asleep it must be folklore must be true.
Make somebody happy this side of the brain.
Where the sun breaks rocks.
Doesn't take much forest to go deep into itself.
A hundred feet from highway you're jungled.
But where am I when all the trees walk by.

402.
I carried the wrong color but who knew.
I told the truth till it became a lie.
You opened the window the whole day fell out.
Close clustered in her mother's closet she.
Because nothing really belongs to us.
Inside our bodies nothing but our sins.

403.
Catch a fish in the sky that's all.
Read all the lost books to learn how.
Meet me midnight shuttered bookshop.
I'll open the warehouse of the uncreated.
Read you for hours from the unwritten book.
What more do you need but me.

404.
Only your habits indifferent you to what I do.
O plea of life small bird so big a shadow.
I see you as you will be I want you as you are.
His blessing not so different from his curse.
This skeptic weather till the door breaks down.
Newton was jealous of the stars.

405.
Why don't they obey me am I not government and law.
When pages move in wind the word shifts too.
When in doubt deliver love to otherland.
A wolf howling from a woman's grave.
Where the god is sunken in the drinker's cup.
The distances between define what places are.

406.
Sun my sister on this aster known.
Squirrels scold in maple's much-pecked wood.
Behind my fox the landscape disappears.
Birdness of forenoon these woods speak deep.
Drink from the silver cauldron of the dead.
Stars float in honey sluggish verjuice of mead.

407.
How do I know when the new becomes.
A million years before this hand still holds.
Not so much as permanent un-beat the poor horse.
The witch has to be the cutest girl in town.
I wanted to know who was hanging in the tree.
I wanted him to speak to me.

408.
In our sad world speak is a copulative verb.
Merlin remembers for me I breathe mere air for him.
But green girl was worth our being here.
Every marriage is underneath the ground.
Lust for meaning is a most do-full flux.
Undo sad heptad week and count by moon!

409.
Finally be cold enough to be a single blue-heart flame.
You were my candle once all wicks away.
I know the meaning of the silver street.
I know where lost things go.
I and not I walked the length of time.
Thrice I called thee before roses were.

410.
O put your opium away and let me sleep.
Beasts wait the last roundup when we're all gone.
They who loved us once demand our absence now.
He told me speaking south the Adriatic coast.
Music's sly geometry compels us to pretend.
Slow as architecture we call this dance.

411.
I give you no context to guess my gist.
So still you understand star sleep.
Lascivious carriage horse in the head.
The horny angel threads our pipes anew.
Disgruntled palimpsests yield revisionist impostures.
How could I think I meant the things I say.

412.
Questionless desires like two harvest moons.
They prey on us as we on little fish.
Angel anglers dangle lines unseen.
They hook us with ideas we're lost.
From such certainties Parmenides was in flight.
Two horses make one single contradiction.

413.
If I say I need you what does that make you.
How can you be a part of my necessity.
These villain names interchangeable wanderers.
The prelate's catafalque among dry-eyed mourners.
Ego death and broth for breakfast new birds sing.
Among all the others waiting to be you.

414.
Close enough to see the ice still green in Labrador.
To see over these trees those trees by Constable.
Unbounded molecular theater we are the shadows.
It's always on its way to end in you.
You is the shallow trajectory of the world's end.
Farmhouse on the moon weird cattle low.

415.
What to do if if turns is.
We run away from morning dew soaks our nakedness.
How dare love before suns rise.
Fill our budget with the wind smells of sea wrack.
Hurry back to the tree thou fallen leaf.
Not even color saves you from yourself.

416.
Colors mean qualia isn't that clear enough.
Name nothing you can't take home.
A word too big to fit a human mouth.
The last name of god is *insan*—there the message stopped.
Fruitflies hover ever round his bowl of peaches.
Long shadows of changing time light is a gong.

417.
Summon them all away from the sound.
Birds' beaks sawing on the house wood.
The sun will fall we'll call it rain.
And if light still travelled but never came.
See far into woods along the sun path who moves there.
There runs a tunnel under everything.

418.
A spell of grace to fall me in your arms.
The fugue runs on empty daylight hungry.
When we're all gone the road runs true.
Translate into tomorrow for me.
In nature's Nazareth where I was born.
They brought me past the shul to autumn.

419.
Heavy traffic of crows I'm telling
What my morning is aren't you glad to know
This much at least of how it was
To be me. The syncope
Of ordinary life. The error
In the weaving is the part of God.

420.
Shifting meters of the measureless.
Bewilder the mind and build the heart.
I just want to watch it rain.
Fire siren not far away who is she now.
Belated owl on the way to need's dark perch.
Or is she standing at my very door.

421.
Let the air move out and in.
Translate this rainwet wooden chair to early Irish poetry.
Before rhyme became unionized.
Until all humans are poets the truth will never speak.
That's what the Bible meant when it still was meaning.
You fly into the sun every night and rise with her a-morrow.

422.
To recognize what pen the poem's written from.
Know which goose in those high autumn vee honks startles

you.

So many trying to be me all right I'll let them do it.
Once in a while win the battle on the hollow moon.
It is like living inside amber.
All these trees and nothing to forget.

423.
Amiable blur of the pyracanthus.
I would have yew all around my house God's acre.
Halfway home is almost gone again.
Half the hurt of sick is hearing the dead call from the wall.
Put a blue stone on every square and see.
Skymaker she does so quietly amend.

424.
One wonders when the other comes to be the one.
I know the names of all those trees *they are tree.*
Enjoy plays where people talk things out.
I will stand for instance here until it tells the truth.
Cars spill music as they pass pollute the rain.
Now you know at last how far away you are.

425.
Every few years the linden blossoms scent the air.
Why not every but morning knows and who am I to reckon.
His *blood streams in the firmament* the stars his sweat.
Green everywhere glimpse of stop sign cardinal glimpsed in
                                                    leaves.
Nature unmans us firmly.
It is big and I am listening.

426.
Home a week and home pure portal.
Coming through the door of your house arrives everywhere
                                                    at once.
In shade behind the yew trees all journeys end.
Nowhere you can't get to sitting still.
You own this world already stop trying to buy it.
Nothing to prove no one to prove it to.

427.
The coffee mill is jammed Duchamp is dead.
We have to do it all again no more irony.
Laughter is the fleer of ruling classes at us.
Irony is society passion is vision choose.
Time-soaked beauty that alarms the heart.
Casper Friedrich praying through his windowpane.

428.
Whizz of high-gear cycle stripping past.
I have thought nothing for weeks I have only spoken.
To speak without thinking gives the words a chance.
Pretend this is flarf then you'll love me.
Packaging rules in this triste colony.
But those are human women on the bikes.

429.
The dead have their own business.
The game is over I am left with full hands.
All my Rachels lost in MoMA's airy chambers.
To be a spokesman for the monster race.
The whole world in flux you too with my desire.
Unlatch the rainbow belt let the sky slip down.

430.
Why build a temple when she stands right there.
Stars up there in blue we see them not.
What I see are bees talking in the linden blossoms.
We know what comes of such conversation.
Strict uncontrived vertical of tree.
She stands right there until you look away.

431.
Those other times we thought were sleeping.
Greenpoint midnight steel mesh of little bridges.
Hope is the subtle poison among the virtues.
Insipid taste of my saliva on my lover's skin.
A shadow moving past the bakery window fearful bread.
Cherry bombs in garbage cans and mothers fretting.

432.
The thought of deity willing and directing this.
This strange play no characters no text.
I dreamt her nuclear in full color held tight.
That dream ended my life all this is ghost march after.
Because we all died then and thought we went on living.
Her snug green clothing and the sky exploded.

433.
Vague she said is beautiful and some birds believed.
How to and not to wear the judge's periwig.
I set this cap upon my locks to set you free.
Maybe that's how all the old days thought.
When you can't walk you must sit.
Bibles are built for such as these.

434.
Am I habit or am I had.
You were my folksman and my judge.
When you moved the world stood still.
Or when you moved you moved it too so both seemed still.
Sequences of things beads of sweat like sequins on your hip.
The dying man hears footsteps on the stairs and they are his.

435.
Music too true to be everywhere.
The nature of sound is to move from center all ways out.
Light seems to be everywhere at once but what does a little
                                                boy know.
When it stops moving they say it stops being.
Hence pervasive Modernist metaphor all art is Dance.
Whence my desire to look into your eyes as you do it.

436.
All the things they mean me to explore.
Empty tomb the nard-soaked cerements.
Now it says me anything again.
To live in silence Athos in a girlless space.
He found the grail and drank from it.
A true Christian rises from the dead.

437.
Or are there other meanings fruited on this beam.
You can't help but elming when the ash is right.
Staring in clear water stone horse trough by La Borne.
Beyond the Boundaries fay women tend to me again.
O Eve me all by yourself and let me still.
Tacit he is quiet and lets the other speak.

438.
All this next part is written in Greek.
High Sumer and the incests rife.
Go down with her to the abandoned gate.
The door swings open and you see yourself.
You stare at yourself puzzled by your seeming nakedness.
Too many opals you think not enough pearls.

439.
In the house on top of the hill a rowboat in the cellar you
                                              never know.
How far does a gull cry fly measure in times of day in colored
                                              clothes.
The door was closed but a mouth said Everything.
Everything you think is yours is everyone's this is history.
Your unarticulated feelings make kings tremble on their
                                              thrones.
Come back when you know how to make the silence speak.

440.
Perception's more like a ship than a marmoset.
It plows through what is there and gets a little wet.
But nothing changes nothing changes.
Waiting long for human certainty the chemistry.
He called me from under the olive tree bitter red stones.
Bale-fires on the landfill hillocks blue.

441.
Gull over grail we have found the right place.
The woods were dark that morning too.
She heard them calling to each other was she one of them too.
You can close your eyes but no way not to hear.
What did they want of her in all that green.
Answers are meetings with no promises.

442.
Wisdom of never crossing river.
How far can you go by land alone.
Once you cross running water you forget all you know.
Wise women stay away from bridges.
Forgetting and forgetting only hold her in his eyes.
The otherness of the other is never other enough.

443.
Every line an argument high school manners of Caligula.
Hurting them past happiness no joy like regret.
But I was in the deep woods that day Morgan assented.
Strapped to a hornbeam tree experiment in control.
She summoned mighty spirits from a breath of air.
And my own breath became the word she says.

444.
The system itself makes villains of them all us all.
Escape the system abandon gain.
Thirty-seven Points of Training the Mind and I am you.
We walked beside me through the woods closer than we can
                                                    ever be.
Of course it's a love song what else do we know how to hear.
Berlioz turned music inward we yearn to be the one we hear.

445.
There is a woods I mean a waiting in half-light.
She'll never show up as long as you keep looking.
Only when your eyes are on the cast of shade or twist of vine.
The forest is the first theater and the last.
Skene the shadow place where everything's alive.
She stands slim as a tree but what she says.

446.
Art makes us interlopers aesthetic awe is fear.
We intrude on masterpieces.
Woe betide the art that welcomes us.
On the marble backside of some chance Venus spent.
The story ever retreating ahead of us leads us on.
Begins and ends *in medias res* we are green without hope.

447.
And in that seminar most she says.
When least dust settles on the humid glass.
Follow wherever it leads and it will you do.
Once I closed my eyes and let my footsteps find the way.
To give yourself unquestioned to the simple seeing.
Behold the treasure house of our differences.

448.
He slept beneath the tulip tree until America.
Her voice woke him saying is where the killing stops.
Every one of us is meant for someone else.
Daybreak but what will heal it.
O she was green and his body filled with her word.
I can't rest in my own old being I must let your voice become me.

449.
Every waking is like this a shattered dark a new-found-land.
At every scale of our perceiving the thing is moving.
To speak stone words without desire.
Desire is all we have and it brings us to the coast.
To want the end of suffering want the children to be fed.
To want shadows to shape letters you can read.

450.
To want things as they are want them to be more than they are.
To want cherries to grow from the empty sky.
To want an answer before the light goes out.
But our conversation is in heaven Saint Benet said.
I am as you made me and I know you not.
I don't know how long anything lasts or you.

451.

Afterludes of DNA our pale identities cascade.
An acid is in everything disposes fate.
But fate means 'spoken' and who can hear that word.
Walk by the marina at twilight garlic aftertaste.
I grew up where the ocean was always waiting.
I stood by salt marsh and prayed choose me.

452.

Let this growling meat of me become your word.
Let me learn it by saying and you are all I am.
Doctors with their fairytales of what goes on beneath the skin.
Nothing's there the body's hollow.
We open the door and see what we expect to see.
The blood-eagle of our ancestors last groan still exhaling.

453.

Choosing the actual tends Vienna dream.
The cemetery shows the names only the names.
All those statues standing in the snow.
In a forest of angels the ones we loved are gone
Noumenal numinous star-shrapnel nominal.
All gone carried off in a river otter's teeth.

454.
We weary players late the outfield think this game still
                                                    beginning.
They never know the names of the names they speak.
Voices *symphonious tremble* in the ancient air inside the stone.
For every word ever spoken lingers in the world in rock in
                                                    wood.
Sometimes the water remembers sometimes crows insist.
You think this fancy I say this science is.

455.
Time to learn another language the one death knows.
We have our trafficking therewith to busy us and soon forget.
For I was born this morning die tonight my true name's
                                                    never.
The lissome lutenist lingers on my lap unheard.
Following instructions I broke the stick.
Praying in the ruined chapel I drank red water from the
                                                    spring.

456.
Crowfeathers business cursive handwriting of the gods.
Yes I believe in them just as I believe in you.
Unlikely other who has such lovely eyes.
I apologize for bringing you into it but what can I do.
Gods peer out at you from your TV.
Legends like maps seduce the unwary.

457.
Wait your excellency the map *is* the territory.
The word is the only thing you've got.
Sligo Somalia Mongolia breath-art of the poor.
Tongue the miracle touch me when you're ready.
It's all in the book already just turn the page.
Writing to the signet for the day of judgment.

458.
Round her neck the whistle turns archers into fallow deer.
The gods work in us by sound.
So many aftermaths so few beginnings.
Now the quiet comes retrieve the spoken wish.
It all is you isn't it once you belong believing.
Color is the radical of gate go through.

459.
The awkward dead accommodate to hidden spaces.
Berlioz wrote down the chorales they complain.
In all aspiring a raft of pain.
But if there's no erasure what can be said.
On living moss they wiped their tender pens.
To fit some new word into all the spoken.

460.
When the wind comes by itself there is no end.
Mother river feeds her infant sea.
Again-bite of inwit Irish women love to disagree.
I saw her sauntering with friends a waft hello.
I watched her from what I called my tower.
A pile of rubble but stood on by none but me.

461.
Asking again the actor slips across the set but sounds.
Hollow places in the earth I fear.
The fairy mound will one day close me in.
Every phobia is rational in the long unfolding of the brain.
Blue flowers grow on lightning bolts come down.
Not every day seems worth its wheels its bronze maiden.

462.
I once lived on earth and learned to talk.
Did I lose the nobility of common speech.
Hills where the Bible hisses like a copperhead.
For vines wander through a house.
What was it like when a wall was just a wall.
Sit in the shed in winter knowing the truth.

463.
Carry home with no rapture.
Grey breezed a green day some miracle.
Partner is a word too easy to be said.
Saying the opposite the other comes true.
Tree time in Barbary rehearse her aquifer.
Treadle the iron footplate that works the mind.

464.

All Venus asked him for were kisses. *(VenAd)*

When you carry your door with you any god can come
through.

Two party system choice naked or veiled rapacities.

I knew you when you spread your will around the room as
wood.

I knew you when the frame was smaller than the picture.

I knew you in the woodwork of your dream.

465.

Wrong move to remember what's wise to forget.

So slowly through these little trees after all breeze knees.

Time for the weather to complain about us.

Weather is the world's response to human will.

Dusty provinces of stale desires.

Those who die in lust are born in sand.

466.

Each life is hell or heaven enough.

Folklore is death's ancient gospel.

How slow the workmen come to doubt the work.

History is the biggest myth of all.

Alpha-males make servants of all the rest.

Nothing else ever happened nothing happens.

467.

The news of the day is pabulum for slaves.
Don't believe a word you don't speak.
Don't think anything's happening but greed.
They give you this to sell you that we're all conspirators
                                                against us.

I chanced on Whitman weeping by the road.
The road goes nowhere I haven't been.

468.

I fell in love with an ever-receding prospect.
The immediate things are the furthest away.
I will never reach your hand who stands beside me.
My legs will never reach the road I'm standing on.
I loved the land when I thought it was for me as part of us.
Now my flag this kerchief starred with coughed-up blood.

469.

Nobody dares to talk this way these days as if it mattered.
Nobody dares to bore you tell what you don't want to know.
You know it all already right as Aristides said.
To ask the question is to stand outside the world.
To answer it connives with tyranny Plato in Syracuse.
Questions are anger and answers are greed.

470.
Be quiet and look at the stupid flower.
What if there really is nowhere else.
Hera ancient Celtic goddess of being where you are.
She gave us folk a yen for contradiction.
The One Who Speaks told Troytown's death.   'Omer/os
Irish women love to disagree again-bite of with-wit.

471.
Or fever spoke then empathy their roar.
The cliffs of Never crumble as we speak.
Crumbling mudstone my thumbnail carved Oregon.
The living image of some words I knew.
The counting numbers gang ancient conspiracy.
Careful how you kiss the wind who will it kiss next.

472.
Cathar politics we need religion to resist authority.
All too soon worship comes to be the magistrate.
Sneak away and do it in the caves and catacombs.
Daytime religion is a thing like taxes.
Only the inner chamber full of bhakti and rebellion
No wonder Jews turn the world off Saturday.

473.
Solemn wrong as a king on his thorn.
O quiet mind my grail my wedding night.
What can that cup be but what she chaliceth.
Baffled by the rings of all connect.
With whom does link not one day meet.
On summer mornings air each mattress out.

474.
Admire me with wagons.
Pregnant I'm from the slightest thought.
The mice of Babylon shun defilements Niddah.
A breeze came and told me I was right.
Wine-colored wall tiles in pre-war bathroom.
The war was coming as it always is.

475.
Quiet in me but not kind I have a jogging mind.
That thy body dare resist my worship so!
What greater thrill for god than worshipping a human
                                                    mortal here
There is no summer here it's all one churning.
Put first the words in place only then define them.
Absence makes white clouds come over trees.

476.
Name the adolescent who dared stroke the word.
In that country no word ever echoes.
It is a property of language not to be gone.
Radical of your eyes forgetting me.
Faithful ships atop the adulterous main.
The bill for all our singing paid by glum Pythagoras.

477.
How strange it is that children should have names.
The uncaught thing the cricket on the kilim.
Night speaks a different cloud outside.
What is that talkative arriving wind.
They say it sucks in from a distant mouth inhaling.
Her sacred lips bespeak a common shaft.

478.
All this becauses nature upon nature
The oily plowman lubricates the furrow.
But then some eider floats bicolored on the wave.
But then the aviator sends mimeo'd poems down the roofs.
But then the children hear me and are afraid.
Latent love involved in mesentery.

479.
Yes you would think a man like me was like me.
No the priest's nightshade shows the wax of scholarship.
You think those are little trees of broccoli.
We are kin to all diseases of the stars.
How else would Romeo come back to life in all that blue.
Grieving is a kind of alcohol your lips are wet.

480.
Crow call my pure oracles.
The insects sing the bowstrings with their legs.
Like the chemical of you it fizzes in me when.
That makes me dangerous romantic dull.
The organ to love you with is language.
Language is the skin of what we think we mean.

481.
Sometimes we think of those we've known or not.
Then there's a holy flurry of remembering.
Getting their names and birthsigns right the color eyes.
Sometimes you make me doubt my good intentions.
I was moral till the bark peeled off the tree.
Then I was ethical as hell and Königsberg.

482.
Anybody who knows land shapes thought is me.
This eighth of a hectare is most of what I think.
Yet I was somewhere else once but was that me.
I am the moss on shabby soil uphill I am the solo buckthorn
tree.

The gods all leave her mark in me.
So much to love so little time.

483.
We need to keep meeting in the door.
Am I done yet the last window open still.
Across the table sad squiggles of an empty pen.
A month away from meaning always.
Get a haircut leave a tip silence is mythology enough.
Suppose *the wrong word* is built into the world.

484.
That axe-cleft gorge they called the Flume.
I am cold there still from the drenched walls.
There is a place before the war begins not me.
To be on the other side of myself.
Maple sugar and pure water I loved her disappearances.
I am the challenge called guessing who you are.

485.
On the day Ts'i they lick other people's skin.
I am the perfect stranger.
Cast the waters overboard the cloud her breath.
The sauntered bumblebee alarms above the book.
My horse stumbled for me *I will not leave this island.*
I am never any closer than you are.

486.
Certain men became bees and entered the hive.
You know them by the hum they left behind.
Their task the drone of human poetries.
Atlantis was built to get them out again.
Ever after we're caught between the hive and the hill.
Nobody home because the city is.

487.
See the city is the primitive accumulation the skandhas

                                              heaped up.
See the city is bricked of happenstance and hope.
The city that I mean the streets are trees.
Only the leaves know how to speak.
The word is my streetcar and my subway snake.
Silent throng one acre thick with metropoleis.

488.
I found a little room in it big enough for me.
Heaven hat and no one hell and a rabbit near.
Willing poverty of thieves annihilating property.
I let you in depend you talk in me.
Sober round-up of all ancient scripts.
Relics holy her scarf her mango stone her word.

489.
Not good at knowing my place the edge of things.
You have all the details already all you need's the tune.
History is all the notes without the score a sack of quavers.
They buzz near me with their busy suns.
Unrule the evidence till water uphill runs.
In that country birds discourse men are silent.

490.
The poor kept idle the rich invisible who lights the light.
The eye has to keep moving to see clear the eye is animal.
The stars are stairs that lost their eyes no way but keep going.
How low did the fingers search to know your name.
A dragon lives in every woods such love must bear.
Love is supposed to make things happen to the world.

491.
To see at least the morning glimmer.
Seeds glad the heat comes down meets heat arising.
We live in the same house and never meet.
These are surgeries of blue desire.
Play tennis with the blind spots in the air.
Every word is code for something no one knows.

492.
From the wine return its cluster to the vine.
Take it at face value there is no other.
The longed-for workmen never show up.
We live in the same language but never speak.
I just want to know the taste inside your mind.
In ecstasy each leaf forgets its tree.

493.
People are freedom no moving parts.
Children building cabins north of the mind.
I want what you left behind in Brazil your shadow.
Pictures askew on walls torment unbalanced minds.
Each word captures a bird women cycle past.
Tiny human fraction free to sit quiet in the morning breeze.

494.
A thousand novels each one up to you.
Arcane narrators navigating by chapel candlelight.
The morning wants something gone.
A silence I keep trying to answer.
Now leave me out of it and let the language talk.
Maxims murmured by a pond with swans.

495.
The purple lips of Vercingetorix.
My empathy with enemies of Rome.
Too many devils for one little hell.
When poetry is far away from law a new sun will rise.
I keep thinking of things to forget.
A lake lost north in the wilds of remembering.

496.
No link to lead you but liking.
Step stepping stones on stilts negotiate unnatural.
Of course it's a sin that's why it works.
Soft shadows of hot humid day discovered gold.
I am the queen she said of where it went.
It disappeared behind me in a cloak of speech.

497.
It could be India the stone older than the world.
Veda than Edda then the stories stumble out of prayers.
A hero is what's left after the story's told.
We think there is a one it happened to no it just happened.
When you pray you're speaking a long time ago.
Story comes from liturgy the way dreams come from dance.

498.
Someone has to do these things.
Forgive me for being rational instead of thinking.
Crow call is all.
Stop soon to start another thing gods love beginnings.
The first act of an opera is almost always the best.
She forgot his kind of pen could write.

499.
Essence submerges in identity this is hell or hospital.
Who you are is somebody else's mistake.
Mint sings pain away and lavender and comfrey.
Help the Understanders to forget.
High duet of living beings lost in trees.
They remind me of a well a wish ago my pennies thrown.

500.
Take the words away and leave the naked edge of meaning.
For camphor unvirtues all other remedies.
Now bed it down and take the lamp and go sannyasin.
Doubt as deep as deer in woods.
Write her name on ice and who is listening.
Continuity of all things hidden in you.

501.
The weight of words expressed in miles per second.
Dangers of the rapture never far.
Heaven is a house where one thing happens at a time.
Kissing my enemy to sleep.
People who walk inside each other's steps.
Before the sun boils off the clouds.

502.
Flagbearer braving into the dark.
Ride the weathercock keep the wind from knowing.
That cold green land up there I only labor for.
Seer salt immaculate lines in her palm.
Thrill of sea all edge and tangency.
Why can't this book be every book and is.

503.
Denser as you go in light let through leaves.
Sabbath pictures turned to the wall.
Our bodies remember Zion never give anything up.
The bones are the last to learn to dance.
I am Baron Saturday my feet are small.
He knows the grail is just behind the alphabet.

504.
Americans easily fooled look where we came.
Find a cathedral worth praying to.
Who are your gods America.
Gladder to smile by the wall and speak the dance.
Migrate from somewhere no wonder we're angry.
Some say architecture is the body of god.

505.
Here is a stone floats in the air makes men kind.
Soon come to the end of the evidence.
Egregious farm machinery too early.
The natural anger of the working class.
Lynchpin of the loud world mother here.
Delicate travellers swaddled in dream.

506.
Ant carrying leaf scrap doctor leaf home.
They know how to fit together go between.
These things we feel are feelings and they go.
One puff of breath is all it takes.
Deep breathing of educated citizens art enough.
Saying without thinking is the speech of angels.

507.
Simple opposites in an old-time book.
No more bone than a banana yet I please.
Form more than substance flesh is pure swank.
Moist swale of morning a well waits in us.
Log cabin for knowers no one lingers.
Be alone alive one whole day so then.

508.
Par ma barbe je suis trop vieillard pour Paris.   *[Max Jacob]*
Maybe I was waiting for you once in a peignoir.
Waiting for the next rhyme the heart grows weary.
A poem gets lost in adoration.
Do I have room for anybody else?
Cathedral of Amiens across my private plain.

509.
What a strange letter little j is think what it spells.
Now I am a telephone now the morning rings.
Disciples gawping at a sky he's not there he's here.
They have always been here the sky is an illusion.
Blue witchcraft and heart full of love.
The heart of sky is in your breast.

510.
Buy two notebooks fill one weigh both to find what writing
                                                        weighs.
Weep from the bridge in white and red the one he wed.
So few stories so many told.
Build a house out of color alone.
The clouds are all recycled breath.
Why does or doesn't everything fall down.

511.
Number is the chiefest of earth's accidents.
How many leaves on just one tree each food a remedy a shade.
Be comfortable Majesty with my nowhere.
Jewish poets on Chinese rivers alter genesis.
Bikes flash sun and shade but woods still seem.
What do morning runners actually think.

512.
All that was purgatory this is bliss.
You rise into the present absolute a cat in your arms.
Midnight full moon a field of fireflies talk leads us on.
And everything meant you then.
And me to do it quick as ampersand.
Things on pilgrimage to be me again.

513.
All the litmus tests are wrong every chemical gives blue.
They all want you here where need aligns with will.
Hot night yew tree medicines something to the air.
Save every living being walk the dotted line,
Invisible voices in the trees perennial theosophy.
They walk so very far to come so close.

514.
Car dragging muffler uphill music everywhere.
In the mind's eye the moon is a cat in her arms.
Animals bring disorders into spotless lives.
Every pet you get a little suicide.
The waltz of trust no one love them all.
A part of every lineage you linger free.

515.
Some people can't help raining.
Weather is a province of the soul.
We want to drench the secret places of those we know.
It's easy to kill said Karzai everybody knows how.
But baffle the rich and succor the poor that's hard.
Arjuna Gunnar know heroes best by what they say.

516.
Could that whole war have been Achilles' dream.
They fight from dawn to dusk as if it were a work they do.
When moon is almost full some mercy lingers.
How many crows taught you that.
What we need to know is how the old names *sounded*.
A kind of searching and a mind to mean.

517.
If we could say the Name in the first tone.
Now we refer but then we could *call*.
There is a tone or tonor in the telling counts.
No prayer goes far without its tune.
When we sing it know what the name means.
What does it mean to be on time.

518.
On blue couches the probe of question lingered in you.
No more stale theogonies the back is as true as the front.
A steelyard swings in the stonemason's court.
Why is everything heavy why is gravity still here.
What kind of force is it never answers never moves.
One or many still can't decide I am that hammer.

519.
Certain wise men planted grass seed on the moon.
Chemistry comes close to the real but cannot speak.
When we were Egypt we knew the shape of things.
Women rule by balancing the kidney region holy slope.
Somewhere far they worry the world.
And Robin soon will make amends.

520.
She will not stop till she's pictured everyone.
Spintrian postures of the desiring mind.
Thrilling nature of unnatural things.
Wake up and persuade them who I am.
Mumble Sanskrit in each other's mouth.
The intimate disorder of being anyone.

521.
Drunkenness a syntax of its own the sober con.
No art is safe from us we spend in everything.
Construe me with the grammar of your hands.
She shot an arrow years ago still flies in me.
To touch the intact and borrow its purity.
I can't guess the other side of where I am.

522.
Why else would anyone be when.
Masterful facecloth dislodges earnest sweat.
Arrogant courtiers chastened by art.
Allein, was tut's I have kissed my mouth and am silenced.
Doctors for the living lawyers for the dead.
I stood before Anubis and he wept.

523.
I names a virtual presence a grammatical tool.
I am not who you think but who thinks you.
Language seeks ways to be somewhere else.
Scapular damp with sweat Francis speaks Wolf.
Wash your mind in any sea you find.
Willing victims of music's importunities.

524.
Every line must be studied both in its place and on the prowl.
A cabinet of curiosities compare and feel fear.
Carry the line with you until it runs out.
Keep me out of mind as long as you can.
To see anyone at all is a dark connection.
To dream of someone is Greek tragedy.

525.
I've said it before so I'll say it again.
The endless knot illuminates relationship.
Be not distracted by the sap of trees.
You can escape from everything but images.
Assume a constant measure and dance to it.
I have seen you silver under ancient arches.

526.
You can't treat a human like that.
Same red meat under everybody's skin.
Read a sandbox in your children's eyes snakeskin by the well.
I went to turn on the street and then the tower fell.
No one remembers and that's the whole story.
We make something else up all the time.

527.
This is a fugue on every you and some and me.
Four voiced doxology of Quaternion itself.
Svabhavikakaya empty hands hold everything.
Allow the actual word for once.
Crystals of blood preserved from wound.
I was with Lincoln last night in his agony.

528.
Things the peaceful mind knows how to see.
You let me hear my mother's voice again.
Younger than I was and with a taste for eel.
No one understands what no one says.
Her time had come upon her then.
I speak a hundred years from her silenced me.

529.
Riverboat rapture no corn for seed our empty shoes.
Why didn't you know these things when you were me.
Rose of Sharon blossomed love made us yesterday.
Old America and we two the only people in the world.
Lakes betray us by showing our reflections.
The sea annihilates such shallow identities.

530.
Something of me I don't know how to give.
To use to say to be too much to me.
Mating customs of these morning shadows.
Amplify the screech Lilith in the nighttime day.
I speak a language no one knows not even me.
I go to a church that has no roof no altar and no god.

531.
I listen to music that has no sound.
I tell stories that have no heroes and no end.
I point fiercely to things that aren't there.
High on my tower a clock with no hands tolls.
I am trapped on the other side of what I mean.
Stop me before I tell you all too much.

532.
Recite the names of flowers and why not.
I am here for you and not another.
Lily rose of Sharon all my living daughter.
Just the ace of you and such round arms.
The Beloved *must* withdraw at times to let you love him.
Elsewise you're swamped with him in pure receiving.

533.
I am quoting from a book I never opened.
Petal from an unknown flower blossoming nowhere.
Plagiarism is the heart of human speech we say what we
                                        hear said.
I thought I saw her moving through the trees.
We are shaped and shorn by how much we know.
From the Antipodes white bird come replying.

534.
There is coming back to be done.
Barley in the malt house nudes on the roof.
I tasted nothing but my vision swam.
Green limestone pools where calendars are drowned.
Came visit from the sky and fed from her lap.
When clocks break time goes on he looked to see I
    understood.

535.
Took me so long to get home here I am.
Waited for the stagecoach in Times Square.
The shape of it shows through no matter.
Sat in the corner of the stair on Coleridge's chair.
When you're on time's side it lets you do.
I shared a cigarette with Charlemagne.

536.
I also am a kind of myth a dynasty misplaced.
Speaking fills up an absence from the world.
I am long-winded as the wind must be.
I was the one who touched you in the dark.
I'll never tire of telling me about you this means poetry.
The wind wakes up like an uneasy dove.

537.
The size of a thing goes by.
Changes carve the clifftops the moors grow greener.
The humid path leads all the crevices of Eden licked.
When we kissed the lips that kissed the Lord's lips.
Secret First Century cenacle the wine was their bread.
They licked it from her nipples till all Rome trembled.

538.
Listless air bereft of messengers.
Time one in Athens and we stuck right there.
The dialectic is a shyster's brief for war.
Men speak dreams men do illusions.
Blood soaks every road we go.
The stink of fantasies spilled into the ground.

539.
Are men the toxins in a blameless earth.
Shaman torn between two evils use one against the other.
All those who know are silent.
No names the flower knows.
Learn from everyone a kayak in your head.
Gym filled with agonized voluptuaries.

540.
I can't stop telling what I barely know.
At a glance the long unnecessary road.
Horns above doorstep monkey in a mountain window.
All this in eye-blink change slippery trombone.
Big rose for such a little tree.
You carry the sun but the moon carries me.

541.
Harmonielehre I hear what I want it to do.
I crave ascending ninths her breath is there.
Then they look like morning glories alas are pink.
A.B.Klein all sound to color gone Thomas Wilfred Clavilux.
All the colors in the fingers now and none to see.
Curve of street a fling of dust and Nazareth.

542.
How to know when things are done.
The empress's last breaths a rosary.
Black roses round oval scutcheon framed.
And this child answers not time's telephone.
Shingled beach seeps sea back in.
We can't be sure this moon will ever set.

543.
Poltroon scavengers of decent labor kapital.
All your blunt perversions needle twist.
Broken-hearted ranger ma'am is am.
How do we know about anything a tune.
Habit of having thrill of letting go.
Win once lose a thousand times a name.

544.

The sky keeps ringing seldom we answer.
Name the wicked things the man has done.
The crows call from the oak top counting my sins.
Never applied for a job never hated my boss.
Effortless hard work what do I know about life.
Only the yellow silk kerchief tied in her hair.

545.

Yesterday he whistled up the wind some came.
As the crows cawing scattered morning cloud.
If you can tell birdsong from sunlight your eyes are too keen.
Dunamis the resting power some passerby deploys in me.
At table one hot night they were talking Aristotle.
The rice listened patiently salt thought about riper melons.

546.

When the mother silent all these years begins to speak.
She speaks through the hands of *certain ones* who know
                                        without knowing.
A new twist on death a mother tells.
She has been through all and all a mother knows.
What happens when she begins to speak.
Is there after all an actual story begins to tell.

547.
The glass in the window discovers and protects.
Soldiers asleep under the horizon.
Quiet factory where children seem to be made.
Even old bricks have words that spell my name.
If you're lucky find a broken abbey.
Facing ancient ruins think: why did I build this then.

548.
What did I have in mind the years made free with.
My arch and time's ivy why did they marry.
Built this church to show what god looks like.
The god seen in dreams had such kind windows.
The rite was for the sake of the stone to help it stand.
Silence makes a house fall down I did all this.

549.
Architecture in fact is human speech.
Wander ruined abbey nothing left but the meaning.
They shaped us stones to keep us listening.
After the horns were broken and the lute strings shorn.
Temples are otoliths are stones with ears.
Dearest friend my hand meaning something hurt your lip.

550.
I take the blame for all goes wrong.
My fault the towers and the abbeys fell.
I am ivy and aquifer subtle ground water leach.
I sicken bees and curdle your wine.
Work unintended evil by desire fogged.
And then the wind winds down my work.

551.
It is not a small thing to be ready to go down.
Ant on my ankle and the sun too hot.
No it is not the sun it is the earth that heats.
Look away from temperature to the tempering inside.
I believe in weather because it's always talking.
We who live for feeling are punished by what we feel.

552.
Not inside me but inside it.
This could be a bible of false premises.
When things turn blue it means some other thing is listening.
Lead in the crucible halfway to silver one nature shared.
Over curtained windows shadows pass this is human language.
Someone is always in there they won't say who.

553.
If I could say it all again it won't be righter.
Places have power by place we live.
Mountain spring we least of beasts attend.
High ceremony of bending low to drink.
Why are we always so far from the water we are.
Turn away from knowing and just know.

554.
A leaf! me given by a friend of wind.
A word could lift it or let us live.
Gold ring he settled in the stream marrying whom.
Who understands all this blue telling.
Because this is your number too.
And everything worth telling fits in you.

555.
Irony is decent in bad times but we must more.
Only a holy fool would dare to open that door.
We die from doing what we know how to do.
Go through the wall and find all you want it be.
Question it but never let it rust.
Broken pathways to a whole hale house.

556.
Leave alone it will work all through.
Etymology tells Eurasia's secrets well the *field* afar.
So many peoples wandered angry meadows west.
Make things happen between tree and tree.
Are there two organs in this loft two chalices for his blood.
Tears in eyes must be the wind what else could it mean.

557.
Rose of Sharon profligate it's all this canicule.
Flowers of heat one for each letter of the alphabet.
They blossom without moving though the wind moves.
Yellow silk around love's hair the precious jewel.
What do the letters say the alphabet says everything.
They say without meaning though their speaker means.

558.
No I think the single letters say all we'll ever mean.
Alphabet a radical taxonomy we have just that many
                                                     categories.

Children's blocks are the real molecules.
In slipshod dreams we waste our tragedies.
Once my Antigone stumbled at my side.
There is no room for us in us the field's too big.

559.
This long sentence of the air they claim is randomness.
A heat wave comes the guilt we bear it also tells.
Will you make me think all this is meaningless.
It happens to us we draw the happen down.
Not enough to read the paper not enough to blame.
Epictetus whispers just start again No blame.

560.
But what is it saying this long sentence of the weather.
In what language is the sky written.
Flowers of experience pray always for the next day.
Tomorrow is my afterlife heaven a dew-soaked lawn.
Are you sure there's even this someone who cares.
Abrupt babylons of wobbling desire flare all night.

561.
What we didn't do turns a cool cheek morning.
Do me do me I'm dumb when I can't get started.
Lull the paretic twitches of arrogant scriptures!
Would you live on a planet that has no night.
Manichean climate of the untamed States.
America always the lesser of two evils.

562.
Those who fled from all they knew fled into *ignorance*.
Convicts fugitives failures clergymen slaveowners hurried here.
They brought slaves the dichotomy the two-party system.
Null-choice engrained in national psyche no nation.
No citizens just a prairie of quarrelsome victims.
American politics eternal resentment unappeased.

563.
Who sent me here all of us still stumbling west.
To attend the fox panting in shade beneath the garden bench.
Adore these heat-splayed Sharon roses.
I had a mind but used it.
I must pay close attention to the weather.
Attend each visiting circumstance the tedious angel.

564.
Welcome the shadow cast by something gone.
Odoevskii's sylph glad madness living concentration.
To be normal is diffuse they get you that way.
Concentrate into keen-minded phantasy break through.
Leave godless ascetics to jog their way to gym.
I have opinions about nothing too.

565.
To know the life of a thing by sharing mind with it.
No mine no thine full feel what eye deigns to observe.
All I know is what happens in me when I behold.
By prayerful practice guess how what I see is you.
Hold onto that knowledge the object shares with you.
A footnote from a time when be good meant be aware.

566.
Numb quiver from which the brute thumbs arrows.
Make the poor vote against the poor how democracy works.
What you could be if you stood inside being.
Crawl at last in from the deserts of becoming.
You are the trees now they rub against the wind.
Trees tame the light a song that Xerxes sang.

567.
How can I choose between the dark and the dark.
There are no heroes there is only consciousness.
It's something else not light comes from the sun.
Drink a little every day water from which she rises.
We are not bereft of wit or counsel.
We have a Way here too that owns us.

568.
The highway under ocean runs through our old streets.
A highway empowers where it goes the Tao lives close.
The Way ways us and the stars speak people round us.
We belong to what we taste every day what we touch.
Her clothes exiguous tattooed with leaf shadows only.
Enemy of sunlight wrapped in silk woven from the moon.

569.

In my kiss there is no time she promised.
In the soul of the soul it is to be sought.
It doesn't fly in the storm doesn't get reborn.
It stays a long time like a redwood or a hill.
Day and night it asks you what you think.
You tell it you think nothing but it comes out a song.

570.

Tao nuns dear dear you you talk to rocks.
Fish from the shallows answer what the sea heard.
All beings are part of the machine of earth listen.
I am never far from being you.
We write with our bodies Tao nuns revise.
Passing by they erase the hesitations of desire.

571.

Accommodate the obvious the secret friends will come.
Fauns panting in the wisdom beat out the heat.
Rest after wanting rouse after having.
The way they talk is to make us talk to them.
Tao nuns slip between the weather and the rock.
You shiver at the beauty of their pass.

572.

It makes a song and dance of everything.
Between the water and the fish the wheel and the road.
Crows are vigilantes in this anarch realm.
You can't come easy all the way from sleep.
He finds the girl he lost in everyone.
Through her surely you can come home to him.

573.

The myths are shrouded but the names still work.
Good Friday veils thrown over their luminous bodies.
Back then artists were up to something new.
Now anyone who catches your eye might be a Tao nun.
Listen to their love song wind rain the passing bus.
Priestess of the actual alerter sign shower svaha.

574.

Tao nuns running through the rain.
They wet you as they run they are the rain.
Is it really rain or just a word caught in your thinking.
Gentle rain thou'dst make love on me the world.
All we can do mister is align your syntax.
Words come out of dream and stand there waiting.

575.

The gates of Eden swing broken from their sockets.
Pass in and out at will that is the secret.
The path is forgiving everyone and everything.
This is the liturgy your life's work approximates.
Better or worse we listen to the rain.
You know full well the rose is aftermath of pain.

576.

The theater cracks open and the bird flies away.
Gods of Africa meet Gods of Thule and Greece begins.
How short a mile when you come from both ends.
Soul met spirit and they still remember.
What was that betweenland and to whom did it sing.
Was it sad Achilles first thought death a kind of chic.

577.

Anyone can act my voice I dreamt this part.
Disturbed by quiet sleep rebuked by clouds.
I have never done enough this is me talking.
Me is the one the Parents talk to the world decides.
We choose the ones who choose us carousel.
Showoff moon in Leo larger than life amen.

578.

Now you know who you've been listening to.
Wizard in a shriner's fez wet from the infidel sea.
All smoke and no mirrors mirrors are hard.
I baffled them by sticking to the truth.
I kissed your shoulder and heard a whistle blow.
Our little business part of vast unseen event.

579.

Softness of roses with the hiss of thorn.
I breed them to believe in us as we in them.
Love's neat reciprocals we have cause to doubt.
Hesiod stands in rare snowfall ruing *narrative*.
We come out head first thinking already.
To find profundity break any sentence open.

580.
Pansies in window box cinderblock garage.
That's all the child needed then the alphabet.
I learned everything and knew nothing then the other way
                                                                                  round.
The answer's everywhere the Stone is floating in the air.
The Stone of the Wise *is* air itself just learn to breathe.
I want to make this small enough so you all can fit.

581.
Taste of a thing you wake up needing.
Last port of call last chance to leave a word.
I am a wounded hero carried safe to Afalon.
They will heal me of my cowardice and doubt.
Never send me back to a man without meaning.
Sister remember our father before we were born.

582.
Lofty landfill with blue methane burning off.
Pick any number and divide by me.
He stood in flames like one who has a message to deliver.
We tried to listen but heard only the environment.
In Muir Woods again the spider answered the riddle it is the
                                                                                  sun.
Then the famous moonbeams came and made us hear.

583.

Will somebody please answer the painting on the wall.
We carry you with us in all our future lives.
You don't have to remember the past you're in it still.
You touch the light between my eyes.
Suddenly everything small I hold it all in my hand.
I am held in someone else's hand the fugue.

584.

No names no norms just the *fishy depths of sea*.
Numinous vacancy *nemus* a holy woods.
Leftover language with a billion hearts to fill.
This thing in your hand imagine it in your hand.
Can you feel the vowels of its being there.
The deep sound of what you understand.

585.

Unscroll the sky a different one.
She wore a fox tail to help her run away.
Conscious life means kindness catches on.
These things have left me as their wake.
Years of running on to learn to stop.
Crows reminding raindrops too.

586.

Different things for the same word.
A ghost in the yew hedge you see.
Tribal on its way back to animal.
The veiled woman is the specter of society.
Men bare their heads in certain churches.
Are they letting something in or something out.

587.
Hiding behind roses like so many meanings.
Wanted to embed itself inside the shape.
The contour not the content the world is pure.
The meat inside is food for someone else.
What bread the angels nibble while we fawn.
The fugue is gone only the pilot light's still on.

588.
Jogging past Jesus on the way to self.
Maybe when they arrive they'll find an empty house.
Maybe I'll be there before them baffled as they are.
Sometimes the sacred and the civic are the same.
Outside the city is all the way in.
Wolves follow fleeter prey across the mind swept plain.

589.
Rescue music quick from such blue sky.
The river of sixes flows from Aphrodite's chair.
Special sun that golds the middle of the night.
The cushions on her throne bear marks we learn to read.
Scratches from lovers' fingernails infect with lastingness.
Our human job to finish up what time began.

590.
If the rapture's riven only rain shows through.
On Baltic strand mope happy alone.
Crossed the minefield into East Germany.
So many stories nobody knows.
Land pirates *Nacktmusik* the huldra live in trees.
Some went down into the sea and stay still searching.

591.
The caravan of barely getting there.
Pink rubber patch on the moon old tire dirty truck.
Hastate leaves opposite on flimsy twigs.
People are always looking through that window.
So darkling hard to distinguish in from out.
Laurel leaves share the sense of what you have not yet spoken.

592.
Don't you feel the trees here are waiting for you.
Can't you feel the wood feels you right back.
First agonist jabbers from the flock of silent dancers.
My words are what their bodies make you say.
Rituals of unimpaired civility why do we touch.
What is absent from my body that I crave another.

593.
Contact high vision quest dark doorways.
With so many pleasures who has time for truth.
Refute the universal theology of despair.
The oaths of children spell their whole lives.
Live in a palace with a herd of brindled cows.
The real city belongs only to the poor.

594.
Now you know I want everything.
These rustic lingos plus time's svelte dialect.
Serenading muses by the score no names please.
I was an infidel before I came ashore.
In these woods lost virginity of streets.
So now you can tell the yodeler from his yell.

595.
Nothing could be less enough for thee I strove.
Against the rising of the dawn go limping.
Never a sure foot even a green horn gives milk.
All of this is in the Torah wring it out.
A fortune-teller drunk among blue jays.
I listen to what the linden tells her earth soprano.

596.
These things insist on being told I didn't.
Secret crankcase drives a faltering world.
Need ten miracles a day just to get started.
One is a sparrow fluffing on a rail.
One is a number no one knows but you.
I forget who all you others are tonight.

597.
Sub tiara to the opera to hear the gold come down.
As other as I am wouldn't you like just once to hold my hand.
Just once to kiss the mouth and mute the words.
I wish I could because everything talks me.
Prolific listening sleigh ride of witty fingers.
Dictionary of a language not yet born.

598.
Supererogatory dialects of angels dialects of silence.
Old mare stands in the meadow pale as the afterlife.
So many ones come after me to zero in on what I do.
Palimpsest for all the scraping still keeps declaring.
A word once written can never be unspoken.
Even the smallest woods is forest absolute inside.

599.
Watch the skill late evening sun slides in to gild the trees.
Someone else is always there to witness.
What we do is not done what we forget keeps happening.
Spiderwebs attune angelic eyes to human art.
Purpose of nature we look becomingly at what we see.
Inhabiting the object with undistracted sense.

600.
If I can only help you see the rose again.
The world was what they told me and no more.
A murky glance a child in grown-up clothes.
Writing in the dark turned night to day.
But she was always there before me so far away.
I found the seam the mother said and opened it.

601.
Impulsive impatient not much time is left.
The old man laid his hand along her thigh.
Jupiter I am he said and weary of the sky.
All I am is young she said and he said that will do.
I'll teach you all my everything I barely know.
Only keep vigil with my dying senses.

602.
Who is the visitor sinks down on our doorstep.
So many lives around us close don't think about it.
From such trees anything might come walking.
If it has legs it loves me.
Do they come of their own or do we summon them.
Some beast rank with death lies down there.

603.
If I had one more I would have none.
My father bore me when my mother windowed.
I see by night and doubt by day.
It is never enough to be rational you have to be there.
Solve the dappled pattern each tree composes.
A task for Bruckner who knew it from inside.

604.
Broken footsteps fill a chalice.
I spoke to the desert itself a hawk cried thrice.
They are coming for me now the clouds.
Language tells you everything I don't.
The wrong is as telling as the right.
Help me out of these soiled opinions.

605.
Sometime tell you what I really mean.
Two voices twine together and that is meaning.
Long after we've stopped talking.
Voices know how to do that leave them to themselves.
Weaving and propagating and telling new lies.
One night you'll hear my voice but you'll be speaking.

606.
In the Temple of the Mother no sunlight comes.
Mirrors shepherd the light this way out of us and in.
We only see what comes from hidden local fire.
We thrive from what winter wheat grows from.
Language is the opposite of land as woman is of man.
Solve et coagula alchemy makes landscape talk.

607.

Moon on park bench sun on sapling fence.
We are not sure of how our children come.
Do you break the rock to make it speak.
That it's all about house and who happens in.
House this hollow seed from which we grow.
How can you tell a mother from a house.

608.

If I had as many lives as there are letters.
Blue jays come close to chide our atmosphere.
Day allow a leaf us dragonfly my arm.
They are coming back now the living ones or always here.
Call it the return cat wolf fox bear wild boar.
Serenity of vultures knowing circles overhead.

609.

Pick one to deceive me all the saints have gone.
Of course the Middle Ages never ended.
Beneath the plum tree a lean fox spits out pits.
Can I walk with you where such people seem.
We are their never-ending conversation listen to us.
Great before ones murmuring their remembereds.

610.

Cool in the trees take off your semaphore and sign.
Feel forward into that vortex between is you.
And every gap an eye and every eye analysis.
It is not good to linger in this place.
The lady left her footprint here and gone.
We are citizens of her absence.

611.
Waking for the cause the yellow rose she answered from.
All texts are one they cry from common pleading.
Deliver from the death and into meaning.
That's enough silence all the rest is being.
You measure it with shivers and avowals.
Arousals he said and the door flew open.

612.
Here we are in heaven are in hearing.
Daily practice of heaven this knowing.
Speedwell summer still and roses after.
Then time began with all those brittle flowers
But it must be daily practice.
What does not today does never.

613.
Every now and then the world appears.
Then there is trembling here and dancing there.
Before you know it the knots come untied.
Your shoes go out walking by themselves.
Your skin persists in nakedness the clocks stop.
Clouds go back to the beginning words they spelled.

614.
Hush the mother says or father will wake.
Hear this basic message of the earth.
Amuse yourselves without annoying Majesty.
Take it any way you like but just take pleasure.
Pleasure is the hardest pill to swallow.
There must be more to me than me.

615.
Dark memory of your children far and near.
For I was the father and I never knew.
I was mother she looked the other way.
Hurt none help all and know your mind.
Nothing else will spring us from the trap.
O chant of prisoners o raiment rent.

616.
Remonstrance May wine and fleecy clouds.
Tear right through them to the blue of truth.
Answer me again before I ask.
Hummingbird on South Bay marsh way to you.
Haunted sex of knowing everything.
Exhausted saxophones scissors fall from thumbs.

617.
Are you really that angry are there lilies too.
Skip every other word and read the truth.
As if lost in the world grieve our absent wood.
By the late night store the god's loud *thiasos*.
The danger of their rapture all could seize.
The way young skin cleans itself of all who look.

618.
So there I was at the head of the stairs.
And they knew me there as one of them.
You have come to the landing from which no one falls back.
I believed her cold fingers and shut my eyes.
Every day is longer than the day before.
I can't help this is personal we live the same world.

619.
He begs forgiveness from the grass beneath his feet.
Logs raft down the river the salt mill hums below the sea.
Go down and get it for me your whole life.
In sleep I came to you and knew you best.
Your skin in dawnlight makes me breathe with awe.
Precise beauty of the one who's gone and never gone.

620.
Small birds chirp in the clutter of the everything soon lost.
Time turns the tables where we try to rest our hands.
Something is happening it must be me.
Free of messages the morning yes.
Once he saw a movie of the actual sea.
A flow that seemed no different from the neighbor sky.

621.
We came to Venice to escape from certainty.
Out of the tapestry and into the market square.
The great ships come close to shore you hear them weeping.
You can moor but never land all voyagers are unclean.
We had no room for greatness and cathedrals.
We were Ceres we were Proserpina we loved abandonment.

622.
The rain does not wet the ground.
She opens the door then opens the door.
Up the curvy steps I never left Vienna.
Forget the name loves you all the way to the top.
Now the church is full turn out the lights.
Never a human breath blow out a candle.

623.

Arms of a young woman hover of a bee round a wet rose.
We come out in all weathers I'm allowed.
We are the ones left at the end of the novel.
We wake the allergens of you never know.
Basket woven of live birds: the sun ascends.
Lustful of the last morning gods really are.

624.

Earth a spinning prayer-wheel gives milk the word.
Om Truths the mockers snided but we are.
Your horoscope's a partitur stand up and sing.
A rim of young whom he totters from to be.
Stories the mind tells to keep itself in love with being.
Drinking from a broken cup he made the dead bird fly.

625.

All I want is miracles crow on a roof.
Gull on garbage scow bee on rose the mind on what.
Now no one close enough to hum excuses.
Raindrop on the written page revises me.
We are ink we flow from the Other's instrument.
And when he struck the rock water gushed from his rod.

626.

No sense in blaming us we are the ones who happened it.
Moral woodwork eat your German lesson organ sing.
How can it be so beautiful and me still here.
I heard the staircase close its mouth behind me.
This is Sonora desert far as Canada to be here.
I learned a different way of doing what I never did.

627.
One day the builder lets the building go.
Shape something so the sky will feel at home.
A place that talks to you inside.
To look upon it is to crave a way in.
Now against horizon one person present.
Architecture is the specter of being.

628.
Go and find out what the other said.
Time to pick up tools and work the sky.
A man hides behind the rumor of his death.
No fall-back from a failed exaltation.
All he wanted was to be holy.
Holiness is always the house of someone else.

629.
These are moral matters—no more things.
Pallid light of paradiso objects dissolving.
Can't the thing we know be a gleam without a stone.
Can't the quick idea spill water on your lap.
Tell me about rain said the blind man to the mute.
It only is as far as you can be with it.

630.
Then it was waiting and a motor churned.
But what does all that music move.
Where is there anywhere to go or to be carried.
You know you're close when roses start to speak.
But is it me who hears the things you tell me.
No more things now just saying is.

631.
Desert the crowded theories of the school.
This clutter you call memory.
Pale mind be licit in your silences he said.
There is always someone talking.
The crystal doorway congested with light.
Shoulder your way through another language.

632.
We know where this is going now we went.
I write down all the answers the bee says.
Nose deep into what is most common.
The cistern up the hill gave cold water for my shave.
Mountainside blue with hydrangeas.
Stare at it till it makes you speak we're in the Vedas.

633.
Don't waste new ink on old words.
The painting's light ran down the torn flesh.
We bleed from no wound smart from no blow.
Speechless specters with a yen for what you think.
Tell till your clothes take off's enough.
Time is the garden where the gods are gone.

634.
Why should we answer when they call.
Ancient instincts lead just through birth to one more death.
Sacer out of time's loop all bright apart.
In the face of the Given Other we see the god.
Look in the mirror till you see that face.
Then forget the one who does the looking.

635.
Something was wrong with the waiting.
There are things to tell you I can't write down.
Mercy is near at hand the oldest servant.
Maybe night took it all away and dawn's a different.
It's the grammar has to be holy not the images.
The cock's combs still break the lady's heart.

636.
In the face of the given other we see outside of time.
The changeless nature gleams through our response.
The permanent good is what someone finally says.
Because I meant you and it all is waiting.
I tell just enough to touch your hand.
Let all the words change places till they see.

637.
Eden where words finally get to listen.
I am committed to the distance between us.
Be honest for once and let the children out.
Stylistically transmitted diseases catch your breath.
The long walk by the marina remembers me.
Woods you wander to make the day too long.

638.
Celebration of the unremembered.
In that country they have a feast of the forgotten.
Withered flowers wrapped around a dead tree,
Old avowals are burned in the pyre.
We are letters in a mysterious document.
Worked into stone it takes no time for time to pass.

639.
Knees hurt when you've been gardening the air.
I plucked hard-stemmed words out of what people said.
This flower grows alone in atmosphere.
Kairos the appointed time when God turns into you.
You forget the animal you ever were before.
You were alive at that hour and that is guilt enough.

640.
Running errands that run you right back.
Adoration of the Virgin's Back she faces angels.
Every sound is an annunciation.
I know nothing of the man you say I am.
Two bodies cast one shadow it is the world.
They kissed me and forgot to take the kiss away.

α

ROBERT KELLY began as one of the founders of the Deep Image movement, which he described in a 2006 interview as "the journey to the depths with language as our only tool and music our only weapon."

The Hexagon is the third in a series of long poems, which began with *Fire Exit* from Black Widow, continued with *Uncertainties,* and will conclude with *Heart Thread* (forthcoming) and *Calls*.

Kelly's more than fifty published collections of poetry include *Armed Descent* (1961); *Kill the Messenger* (1980), chosen as the *Los Angeles Times* Book of the Year; *Red Actions: Selected Poems 1960–1993* (1995). *Bookforum* critic Joseph Donahue, praising *Lapis* (2005), noted that Kelly "has given magic back its dignity, finding it in human warmth." More recent collections are *May Day* and the forthcoming *The Secret Name of Now*. He is also the author of several novels and collections of short stories, as well as *Oedipus after Colonus and other Plays*. His collected essays were published in 2015 as *A Voice Full of Cities*.

Kelly's honors include an Award for Distinction from the American Academy and Institute of Arts and Letters and a fellowship from the National Endowment for the Arts. He has taught at Bard College since 1961, where he was a founding member of the Milton Avery Graduate School of the Arts. He is the 2016–2017 Poet Laureate of Dutchess County, New York, where he lives with his wife, the translator Charlotte Mandell.

TITLES FROM BLACK WIDOW PRESS
TRANSLATION SERIES

A Life of Poems, Poems of a Life
by Anna de Noailles. Translated by Norman
R. Shapiro. Introduction by Catherine Perry.

Approximate Man and Other Writings
by Tristan Tzara. Translated and edited by
Mary Ann Caws.

Art Poétique by Guillevic.
Translated by Maureen Smith.

The Big Game by Benjamin Péret. Translated
with an introduction by Marilyn Kallet.

*Boris Vian Invents Boris Vian: A Boris Vian
Reader.* Edited and translated by Julia Older.

Capital of Pain by Paul Eluard.
Translated by Mary Ann Caws, Patricia Terry,
and Nancy Kline.

Chanson Dada: Selected Poems by Tristan Tzara.
Translated with an introduction and essay by
Lee Harwood.

*Essential Poems and Writings of Joyce Mansour:
A Bilingual Anthology.* Translated with an
introduction by Serge Gavronsky.

Essential Poems and Prose of Jules Laforgue.
Translated and edited by Patricia Terry.

*Essential Poems and Writings of Robert Desnos:
A Bilingual Anthology.* Edited with an
introduction and essay by Mary Ann Caws.

EyeSeas (Les Ziaux) by Raymond Queneau.
Translated with an introduction by Daniela
Hurezanu and Stephen Kessler.

Fables in a Modern Key by Pierre Coran.
Edited and translated by Norman R. Shapiro.
Full-color illustrations by Olga Pastuchiv.

*Forbidden Pleasures: New Selected Poems
1924–1949* by Luis Cernuda. Translated by
Stephen Kessler.

Furor and Mystery & Other Writings
by René Char. Edited and translated
by Mary Ann Caws and Nancy Kline.

Guarding the Air: Selected Poems of Gunnar Harding.
Translated and edited by Roger Greenwald.

The Inventor of Love & Other Writings
by Gherasim Luca. Translated by Julian & Laura
Semilian. Introduction by Andrei Codrescu.
Essay by Petre Răileanu.

Jules Supervielle: Selected Prose and Poetry.
Translated by Nancy Kline and Patricia Terry.

La Fontaine's Bawdy
by Jean de La Fontaine. Translated with an
introduction by Norman R. Shapiro.

Last Love Poems of Paul Eluard.
Translated with an introduction by
Marilyn Kallet.

Love, Poetry (L'amour la poésie) by Paul Eluard.
Translated with an essay by Stuart Kendall.

Pierre Reverdy: Poems, Early to Late.
Translated by Mary Ann Caws and
Patricia Terry.

Poems of André Breton: A Bilingual Anthology.
Translated with essays by Jean-Pierre Cauvin
and Mary Ann Caws.

Poems of A.O. Barnabooth by Valery Larbaud.
Translated by Ron Padgett and Bill Zavatsky.

Poems of Consummation by Vicente Aleixandre.
Translated by Stephen Kessler.

Préversities: A Jacques Prévert Sampler.
Translated and edited by Norman R. Shapiro.

The Sea and Other Poems by Guillevic.
Translated by Patricia Terry. Introduction by
Monique Chefdor.

To Speak, to Tell You? Poems by Sabine Sicaud.
Translated by Norman R. Shapiro. Intro-
duction and notes by Odile Ayral-Clause.

Forthcoming Translations

Earthlight (Clair de Terre) by André Breton.
Translated by Bill Zavatsky and Zack Rogrow.
(New and revised edition.)

*The Gentle Genius of Cécile Périn:
Selected Poems (1906–1956).*
Edited and translated by Norman R. Shapiro.

MODERN POETRY SERIES

ABC of Translation by Willis Barnstone

An Alchemist with One Eye on Fire
by Clayton Eshleman

An American Unconscious by Mebane Robertson

Anticline by Clayton Eshleman

Archaic Design by Clayton Eshleman

Backscatter: New and Selected Poems
by John Olson

Barzakh (Poems 2000–2012) by Pierre Joris

The Caveat Onus by Dave Brinks

City Without People: The Katrina Poems
by Niyi Osundare

Clayton Eshleman/The Essential Poetry:
1960–2015

Concealments and Caprichos
by Jerome Rothenberg

Crusader-Woman by Ruxandra Cesereanu.
Translated by Adam J. Sorkin. Introduction
by Andrei Codrescu.

Curdled Skulls: Poems of Bernard Bador.
Translated by Bernard Bador with
Clayton Eshleman.

Disenchanted City (La ville désenchantée)
by Chantal Bizzini. Translated by J. Bradford
Anderson, Darren Jackson, and Marilyn Kallet.

Endure: Poems by Bei Dao. Translated by
Clayton Eshleman and Lucas Klein.

Exile Is My Trade: A Habib Tengour Reader.
Translated by Pierre Joris.

Eye of Witness: A Jerome Rothenberg Reader.
Edited with commentaries by Heriberto Yepez
& Jerome Rothenberg.

Fire Exit by Robert Kelly

Forgiven Submarine
by Ruxandra Cesereanu and Andrei Codrescu

from stone this running by Heller Levinson

Grindstone of Rapport: A Clayton Eshleman Reader

The Hexagon by Robert Kelly

Larynx Galaxy by John Olson

The Love That Moves Me by Marilyn Kallet

Memory Wing by Bill Lavender

Packing Light: New and Selected Poems
by Marilyn Kallet

The Present Tense of the World: Poems 2000–2009
by Amina Saïd. Translated with an introduction
by Marilyn Hacker.

The Price of Experience by Clayton Eshleman

The Secret Brain: Selected Poems 1995–2012
by Dave Brinks

Signal from Draco: New and Selected Poems
by Mebane Robertson

Soraya (Sonnets) by Anis Shivani

Wrack Lariat by Heller Levinson

Forthcoming Modern Poetry Titles

Dada Budapest by John Olson

Fables by Pierre Coran.
Translated by Norman R. Shapiro.

Fractal Song by Jerry Ward

Funny Way of Staying Alive by Willis Barnstone

Geometry of Sound by Dave Brinks

Memory by Bernadette Mayer

Penetralia by Clayton Eshleman

LITERARY THEORY / BIOGRAPHY SERIES

Barbaric Vast & Wild: A Gathering of Outside and
Subterranean Poetry (Poems for the Millennium,
vol. 5). Eds: Jerome Rothenberg and John
Bloomberg-Rissman

Clayton Eshleman: The Whole Art
by Stuart Kendall

Revolution of the Mind: The Life of André Breton
by Mark Polizzotti

WWW.BLACKWIDOWPRESS.COM